BEOWULF

BEOWULF

A New Verse Rendering by

Douglas Wilson

canonpress
Moscow, Idaho

Douglas Wilson, *Beowulf*
Copyright ©2013 by Douglas Wilson

Published by Canon Press
P. O. Box 8729, Moscow, Idaho 83843
800-488-2034 | www.canonpress.com

Cover design by James Engerbretson
Cover and interior illustrations by Forrest Dickison
Interior design by Valerie Anne Bost
Printed in the United States of America

Library of Congress Cataloging-in-Publication Data

Wilson, Douglas, 1953–
  Beowulf: a new verse rendering / Douglas Wilson
      pages cm
  ISBN 978-1-59128-130-6
  1. Beowulf—Adaptations. 2. Beowulf—Criticism, Textual. I. Title.
  PS3626.I5787B46 2013
  811'.6—dc23

                                        2012049259

16 17 18 19 20 21 22   10 9 8 7 6 5 4 3

This book is for Bekah, a blessed dedication.

FAMILY TREES

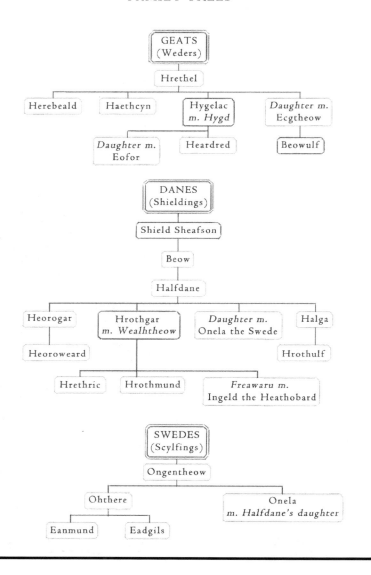

The World of
BEOWULF

SWEDES

Heathoreams

GEATS

Jutes

Skane

DANES   *Heorot*

Eider

Heathobards

Vandals

Gifthas

Wulfings

FRISIANS

Vistula

Hetware

FRANKS   *Rhine*

Meuse

Elbe

/

CONTENTS

INTRODUCTION
—✠ ✠—

Beowulf has long been an attachment of mine, and this book is really a culmination of that attachment, a genuine labor of love. I can still remember the moment in high school when I saw someone's copy of Raffel's translation. I don't remember when I read it first, and I don't know how many times I have read it since, but I know that the poem handsomely repays return visits. Measured by C.S. Lewis's criterion in *An Experiment in Criticism*, which is that good books should be revisited often, this poem is in my top ten.

One of the things I must do right at the beginning, I suppose, is explain what I mean by saying that this edition of the poem is a "rendering" and not a translation. I know enough Anglo-Saxon to be a hazard, but not enough to set up shop as a translator of anything so important as *Beowulf*. I know the words *attercop*, which means spider, and *rimcraft*, which means arithmetic, and *merscmealuwe*, which means marshmallow. But unfortunately, none of those words comes up in *Beowulf* really, and so there I am, just sitting there. So a suitable humility for someone of my limited means in Old English means that publishing a proper translation of *Beowulf* is out. I never want to get a phone call from Seamus Heaney inquiring into just who exactly it is I think I am. Who wants to be *that* guy?

So what is a rendering, and why is it any better? While I am limited in Old English, I do okay in New English, and know my way around, both with the regular stuff and in the reading and writing of poetry. So what I did was this. I took about five different translations of *Beowulf*, including my two favorites (Heaney and Chickering),[1] got the sense of lines x, y, and/or z from them, and then cast that general sense into my own modern form of an Anglo-Saxon-style alliterative poetry. Then I did the same thing over again, and went on and on until I was done. Since I was making free to add words for the sake of the alliteration, and because I sometimes supplied my own imagery, the result is a loose paraphrase of the sense of the original and not a knock-off of any of the translations I used. At the same time, the poem can generally be followed "line by line," give or take a couple of lines, and I am not saying I *never* looked at the original. What with one thing and another, this version of the poem has three more lines than respectable editions do. I don't know. It was dark. They were big. Just think of it as more *Beowulf* than you would get with those other editions. But the sense of the original is there.

It would be as though someone decided to take five different modern translations of the book of Job and use them as the basis for rendering the whole thing into an epic poem of rhymed couplets. I am not saying that this would be a good idea, but it gives you the general idea of the process that went on here. When you were done, it would kind of hard to identify any of the translations though (hopefully) it wouldn't be hard to identify the fact that it was supposed to be the book of Job.

For example, for line 11, I have,

> Gold came, and glory . . . a *good* king that was!

Heaney has,

> and began to pay tribute. That was one good king.

---

1. Here's a list of all five: Seamus Heaney, *Beowulf: A New Verse Translation* (New York: W. W. Norton, 2000). Howell D. Chickering, *Beowulf* (New York: Doubleday, 1977). Ruth P. M. Lehmann, *Beowulf: An Imitative Translation* (Austin: University of Texas Press, 1988). Burton Raffel, *Beowulf* (New York: Mentor Books, 1963). J. Lesslie Hall, *Beowulf, an Anglo-Saxon Epic Poem* (Boston: D. C. Heath, 1892).

Chickering translated it this way:

> pay him tribute. He was a good king!

The form of poetry I put it into requires some explanation as well. The original poem is made up of lines that are each called a *stich*, and which are broken up into two *hemistiches*. The first stressed syllable in the second hemistich needs to alliterate with the two stressed syllables in the first hemistich. A good example can be found in line 5.

> *Monegum mægþum   meodo-setla ofteah*

The two *m's* in the first hemistich alliterate with the first m in the second half of the line, which set the alliterative standard. As it happens, according to our forebears, any stressed syllable beginning with a vowel counts as alliterating with any other vowel. My father, one of my copy readers, described this as "cheating," but I am sticking to my guns. It may be cheating, but it is an ancient form of cheating, hoary with age. This is the general form I tried to follow so that the reader of modern English would have some sense, not only of the content of *Beowulf*, but also of the kind of texture it had.

Now strictly speaking, this means that each line should have only four stresses, and this is where I fudged a bit. And as much as I would like to believe this was rule-guided behavior, I did this part mostly by ear. In stressed-timed languages (which both Old English and Modern English are) we naturally speed up and slow down as we speak in order to make our words fit within the time allotted. In order for this to work, the extra stresses either have to be muted or placed well. My lines are sometimes a tad longer than a purist would allow, with extra stresses, but they can be said in a way similar to what happens when you say the *monegum mægþum* bit given above.

Here is an example of me being strict with myself:

> Took a maul to the mead-benches, mangled his enemies (5)

And as it happens, that is my rendering of the *monegum mægþum* line.

And here I am being not so strict. The first syllable of *memory* is also stressed, but it can be read as a subordinate stress and (so I think) it all works out.

His thanes thanked his memory, and thought a sea burial (28)

There were other places where I cheated by not having the alliterative word fall on a stress at all—but as Ovid taught us long ago, *Ars est celare artem*. It is art to conceal the places where you jiggered it a little bit. I also made the *g* in Geat (Beowulf's tribe) alliterate with a hard *g*, and not with the way they likely would have said it back then. So if you read this poem aloud, you will need to say *Geet* and not *Ye-aht*. So sue me.

Some editions of *Beowulf* have a space between the two halves of each line (it is called a *caesura*). We decided against that as a visual distraction, and because the alliteration should make it possible to identify the two halves of the line without the space. The reader may stumble over some lines when they are read silently, but if they are read aloud (as the poem was originally intended to be read), the internal logic of these rhythms will become apparent, at least most of the time. Another reason for such variations from the norm is that strict adherence to the form could result in something entirely too sing-songy, which in an epic could become an affliction around the two thousandth line. Keep in mind also that the alliteration may come in the middle of a word. To make up an example here, *returning in triumph* alliterates.

Another staple of Anglo-Saxon poetry is called the *kenning*, which can best be understood as a compressed metaphor. Some of the original kennings are found here along with some new ones that I contributed. For example, the ocean was called *hron-rade*, or whale-road. The human body was *banhus*—bone-house. The sun was the world-candle, and so on. I wanted the reader to have that particular experience in reading the poem as well.

The poem was originally broken up into sections called *fitts*. I renumbered the fitts for reasons that are explained in the second essay, and I entitled them to make the chiastic structure of the poem clearer.

The point in doing all this was to give the modern student a general experience of the storyline while at the same time providing a very close approximation of the experience of Anglo-Saxon. Whether that happens or not is out of my hands now, but one still hopes.

Douglas Wilson

BEOWULF

✠ ✠

Section 1   1 - 1250

FIRST FITT † *Funeral of Shield*

Hear the song of spear-Danes from sunken years,
Kings had courage then, the kings of all tribes,
We have heard their heroics, we hold them in memory.
Shield Sheafson was one, scourge of all tribes,
Took a maul to the mead-benches, mangled his enemies.
He rose and in rising, he wrecked all his foes.
A foundling at first, he flourished in might,
A torrent of terror, war tested his mettle.
So he bested and broached the borders of nations;
The whale-road was wide but his warriors still crossed it.   10
Gold came, and glory . . . a *good* king that was!
So Shield had a son, sent as a gift,
A cub for the courtyard, a comfort from God
For the nation had known long gnawing of troubles,
Great trials and tempests, long times of deep suffering.
They were left leaderless so the Lord of all Life,
The great glory-Ruler, gave them a chieftain.
Shield's son he was, and summoned for glory.
Beow was brilliant, a banner of northernness,
The pride of great princes, the pride of his family.   20

So warriors in warfare must be wise in that way
As ring-givers rise they reach their companions
So later in life they won't be left on the field.
His thanes will stand thick with him, there battle is joined.
Such generous gifts are good for deep loyalty.
Shield was still strong when summoned in time,
This Dane-king departed to death—the Lord's keeping.
His thanes thanked his memory, and thought a sea burial
Would keep the command their king had passed on to them.
30 To the shore of the sea they shouldered the burden,
Committing the king who had covered his people.
Silent, sheathed in ice, the ship rode the harbor,
The ring-prow was ready, and rigged for the journey.
They laid out their lord, beloved by all of them,
Amidships the mast, they remembered and placed
Treasures and tackle and trust most of all,
Battle gear, blades edged, and bright gold and silver.
Prestige presided there, piled honor on deck,
I never had known a north ship so fitted—
40 The weight of that wealth, and the warriors whose tribute,
Would sail with this ship with it sent far away,
Their purpose presented to the power of the flood.
They decked out his death and dealt with him bountifully,
No little gifts, no less than left in his infancy,
When set adrift on the sea, a sent-out waif,
They left him lonely, lost but for destiny.
They set high the standard, a standard of gold
High toward heaven, with hearts full of grief,
The ship they let slide, to sea it departed.
50 With minds full of mourning, no man here can say,
No wise one, no warrior, no wizened hall bard,
Can see or can say who will salvage that treasure.

Second Fitt † *Hrothgar rises, Grendel stirs*

So Beow then built some battle-strong towers,
Admired and esteemed, an able Dane king,
Through long life and rule when left by his father
To *his* rule and reign and his right to the throne.
Then his heir, the great Halfdane held sway in his turn
As long as he lived, their lord and their elder.
He was father to four, this fighter and chieftain.
One after another they entered this world,   60
First Heorogar, then Hrothgar, then Halga the good;
Then came a queen, future queen for Onela,
A balm for the bed of that battling Swede.
Then Hrothgar held firm, held victory in battle,
Friends flocked to him, foes fled from him,
And mighty his men grew, a masterful army!
So a command came from him, the king thought to build
A royal hall, rising in fame, erected by guildsmen,
With gables and glory and greatness forever,
A mead-hall, a marvel, for men to speak of forever.   70
There his throne would be, and thriving with gifts,
He would give out those gifts, all God had bestowed—
Kingly gifts, but no common lands, or cruel giving of souls.
This hall, I have heard, was a haven for craftsmen.
Through middle-earth, men were summoned, making way to the building.
Soon it stood, magnificent, and soon glory rose.
Finally finished, in full view it stood,
The hall of Heorot, as he spoke the name,
The worthy king had willed it, whose word was law.
So he kept his kingly word and came with rings,   80
Treasures, and torques, the tables were heaped,
The hall reared up high, with horn-gabled corners,
Baiting the battle-flames; that burning would come.

Hatred for Hrothgar was held in abeyance
But a son-in-law soon would bring samples of rage.
Now a demon demented, in darkness a prowler,
Held a hard grudge when he heard with great pain
The great and the good with glory were feasting,
The scop[2] sang their songs, and the strings were well played,
90 The harp filled the hall, a herald of joy.
So skilled in his singing, he sang the creation,
The Almighty had ordered the earth to be fashioned,
Shining, the single plain surrounded with waters.
He summoned the splendor of sun and of moon,
Lifting as lamps their lights for *earthwaru*.[3]
He filled all the fields with fruit for the tasting,
He gave us such greenery, good leaves and branches,
And made man and beast that all move in His quickening.
The place was full peaceful, and pleasant for men
100 Till finally a fiend, fresh out of Hell,
Began to give grief with ghoulish, wild haunting.
This grim monster was Grendel, gifted with terror,
Haunting marches and moors, marauder of villages,
Malicious and miserable, in marshes he lived
For some time with the terrors, the type who were banished
By the Creator, as kinsmen of Cain, who had blood on his hands.
The Eternal Almighty had everlasting vengeance for Abel.
Cain had gotten no good from his grasping in envy
For the Lord of all life from the light drove the kin-slayer
110 And he went far from all friendship, into fens of dark exile.
He was the father of phantoms, and far from the living,
Begetting ogres and elves and evil black ghouls,
Giants defying just Heaven, the Judge of all mortals,
Until the time came for the Titans' great judgment.

---

2. A scop is a court singer/poet.
3. A back coinage from *helwaru*, meaning inhabitant of Hell.

THIRD FITT † *Grendel kills thirty men, Heorot deserted*

Quietly night came, and, creeping, Grendel as well,
To spy out the safety of the soldiers' great mead-hall,
To see how they slept after savoring beer.
Great nobles were nodding and never disturbed,
Lost to sadness and sorrow, summoned in peace,
Dead in their dreams. The damned spirit came suddenly,   120
Furious, fierce, and formidable in anger,
Grim and greedy he grasped thirty men
From their rest and he rushed to the refuge of home,
Flushed in his fury, inflamed in his hatred,
The bodies he butchered, in bulk he took them.
The grim dawn's gloaming light gave to disaster,
The depth of destruction was done and forever.
Wails from warriors, their weeping was heavy,
The morning for mourning, their mighty chieftain,
So long their leader, so lifted by grief.   130
That strong king suffered, stricken with sorrow,
He thought of his thanes, he thought on their loss,
Aghast at the ghoul's carnage, grieving his men,
He looked on the loathsome tracks left by the monster.
He was stunned, struck numb, but severed from hope.
The very next night their nemesis came back,
Striking again, slaughtering more, savoring murder,
Malignant, malicious, no remorse for his sinning.
So then the thanes shifted, the thanes moved their bedding,
Seeking rest somewhere, somewhere other than Heorot,   140
Sleeping in some of the scattered outbuildings.
Who but the blind would bed down in *there*?
Who could not conceive that conqueror's deep hatred?
Whoever escaped kept always away.

So Grendel in greed held goodness at bay,
One against all, that one against many,
Till greed toppled greatness. The ghost hall, deserted,
Stood wasted twelve winters of woes in their seasons.
The Shielding lord suffered, his sorrows were deep,
150 In terrible torment, his torment in grieving.
All tribes heard the telling, and retold the lays,
Sad mournful music of the murders of Grendel,
How Hrothgar was hated and the hall was deserted.
The feuding ferocious, the fighting was spiteful,
Nothing but war, nothing, and nothing but battle.
No peace and no parley, no peace-price accepted,
The Danes must all die, he dealt nothing but anger.
No herald could hope to hold an agreement,
Given as gift by those gut-bloodied hands.
160 Instead the sick monster would stealthily wait,
As darkened death-shadow, a dim ambuscade,
Waiting for warriors, a wicked hot malice,
On moors that were misty, where men cannot know
How these whispering warlocks, these wights from Hell glide.
So crimes he committed, cruelties plentiful,
That fiend in his frenzy, that fiend in his hatred.
He made Heorot his home, haunting at midnight,
Ghostly and gliding in the glittering hall,
But the thought of the throne was a thought filled with horror,
170 He could not come near it, that outcast and outlaw.
Heartbreaking hard times were these held by the Shieldings,
Their princes, their planners, their powerful counselors
Would come offer counsel to their king in his grieving,
Plotting and planning their path of resistance,
How best to give battle with brave men and warriors.
Weary, they wavered at times, worshipping idols,

Summoning sacrifices, saying old words aloud,
Praying the demon who damns would deliver them.
Old customs were curious but comfort was missing,
Their hope was in Hell, and their heathenish ways,   180
In dire need and deep thoughts they did not know God,
The Judge who loves justice, who judges our deeds.
The High King of Heaven, the holiest one,
Was not known to them though they needed His wisdom.
Cursed is the coldness of comfort deceiving,
That thrusts a poor thane in a thicket of fire,
Forfeiting help and forgiveness forever.
But blessed is the man who busy in prayer,
Can deal with the dying and deliberately seek
The Father's great fellowship and final protection.   190

FOURTH FITT † *Hrothgar broods, Beowulf sails and meets the coast guard*

In that troubled time the trouble continued,
No stop to the sorrow and steady affliction.
So soon Halfdane's son had strife far too great,
Night terrors, night panics, and never a respite
From the cruel spirit's spite and sputtering envy.
But home in his haven, Hygelac's thane,
A good man, a Geat, heard of Grendel's deep malice.
Strong-minded, the strongest of all sons of men,
In his time, battle-tested, he was tried and was ready.
High-hearted and huge, he held out the order   200
To fit and to fashion a famous wave-cutter,
To sail the swan-road to serve the Dane king.
No sage tried dissuade that savior from going,
Though dear and devoted, they did not deny him.
They wrestled to reach, they read all the omens.

That mighty man had measured recruits,
The best from all battles, the bravest of Geats,
Stalwart and strong, the strength of their nation.
He tested and tried them and told them his mission.
210 A captain courageous, a clustered fifteen,
Skilled at the sea toward the shore they went down.
The time quickly came, the quest had begun,
The ship was soon set, settled by cliffs.
Men soon gained the gangway, their gear was then stacked;
The eddies edged the boat, they entered with weapons,
All mounded amidships, hard metal bejeweled.
They shoved off and sailed, they sailed to their journey,
The sea willing and waiting, a ship well-braced with timbers,
To open sea, across salt water, they accepted their task.
220 The foam flocked her neck, she flew like a bird
As they sailed the sea gray, at the second day out.
The curve of their cutting prow, the carving of water,
Such that they saw land, these seafarers sighted it,
Sunlit crags, silvery cliffs, and shores with steep rocks.
Landfall at the headlands, and a looming bright shore.
The deep sea was done, that deed was behind them.
Voyage done, they vaulted over the rail,
And stood on the sand and savored their landing.
They moored and made fast, their mail flashed and clattered,
230 They thought to give thanks, with thanksgiving to God
For a smooth and silent wave-road, for a simple crossing.
A watchman waited, a warrior of the Shieldings,
Whose duty was diligence every day on the sea-cliffs.
He saw their gear glinting, down the gangway they passed it.
His desire burned deep, that devoted sentry,
Hrothgar's fine horseman held his spear out,
Riding down at the ready, they would reckon his challenge.

His manner was manly; his message was formal.
"What has the wave-road brought us, what warriors are you?
Your coats speak of combat, your courage is open, 240
Glinting with gold, must we guess at your purpose?
Your high ship is here with your hull on our beach.
A sentry and sea-watch stands silent for years,
Long have I held watch as Hrothgar's coast eyes,
And never have known such nobles to land here.
I guard against greed with great armies behind.
Never before, never so brazenly, have knights or invaders
Carried shields to this coast with questions unasked.
Have our kinsmen consented to your coming this way?
And a mightier man, massive and strong 250
I never have known. He is no mere retainer,
Dressed in such dread and deadly fell armor.
Your lineage, lord, give me leave to request it,
Before leaving your boat to begin your way inland,
I must know your mission, your men and homeland,
You strangers and spies, scouting out our own Denmark.
I ask then again, this ocean brings aliens.
I seek what you say, the sooner the better,
It is best to be brief before more time passes."

FIFTH FITT † *Beowulf answers the coast guard*

Their leader unlocked the lid of his word-hoard, 260
And spoke words of silver, summoning wisdom.
"We are Geats, of good will, from a great, far-off nation,
Hearth-men with Hygelac, that high-hearted chieftain.
My father was famous, his fist was renowned,
Ecgtheow, eager for battle, he entered true glory,
He went with his wisdom after long winters extended.

All counselors, with their craft, coveted his wisdom.
They knew him, and knowing, they never forgot him.
Our hearts are not hardened, we hold out good faith,
270 We come to your country, your king, son of Halfdane,
Your shield and your shelter—you should show us the way.
Our mission is not minor. Take this message for your king,
That leader of leaders, the light of the Danes.
No secrets, no spying, we were summoned by trial.
Your terror, *your* trial, that terrible night-bane,
Who ravages this realm, who ruins your feasting,
Some sort of ghoul, a seal on your grief,
With malice malignant he murders your people,
In shame and in slaughter—my service is offered,
280 To Hrothgar my heart, my whole-hearted counsel.
A plan I propose, with purposed deliverance.
Such counsel has come, and keeping with prudence,
If Hrothgar will hear it, he will heal from his sorrow.
If not he will never, benighted and blind,
Get free of that fiend, or follow deliverance.
That coldness and cruelty will keep coming to haunt him,
As the height of that hall rises high up to taunt him."
Undaunted, decisive, the deadly-eyed sentry,
Astride his great stallion summoned an answer,
290 "With stout heart, and sense, you can see right away
The difference . . . distinction . . . between doing and talking.
But I take your tale, your troop is full loyal
To the shield of the Shieldings. Let me show you the way.
With your weapons of warfare, you may walk here behind me.
My comrades commanded to keep your ship safely,
Fresh tarred for the testing, this trial, your mission.
They will hold it in honor, unharmed from an enemy,
Until once again tested, it tries the high seas

With curved prow courageous to carry you homeward,
As heroes, high-hearted, to the homes of your Geatland.
May your courage come with you and keep your lives safe,
The valiant, surviving, and victory secure."
So they set off together, and their ship rode the water,
Broad in the beam, the best of their fleet,
Resting on ropes, riding at anchor.
Boar-shapes in bronze on their battle cheek guards,
Good were the goldsmiths who gave them that fierceness.
Those warriors walked, they went in formation,
Until coming closer they caught sight of glory,
The high-timbered hall, that held their fell mission,
Both good and great, the gilding was splendid.
Men knew what it meant, majesty lived there,
The glint of gold roofing gave out stabbing light.
Their guide, the sea-guard, gave them instructions.
Dazzling but distant, he directed them to it,
The shortest and straightest way, simply to follow.
Then he wheeled and he went, wished them Godspeed,
"May the great Father favor you and find you in kindness,
Bestowing His blessings and backing your exploits.
For myself I must go and make my way back
To the coast where I can keep my watch up for raiders."

Sixth Fitt † *Beowulf and Wulfgar*

It was paved there, and perfect, the path ran on straight.
The men in their mail, marched glinting in sunlight,
Mail hand-linked, hardened, high gloss in iron,
Which sang as they stepped, straight to the hall,
All grim was their gear, and good was their step.
They stacked all their shields, these sea-weary warriors,

Holding that hardwood, on the high wall they leaned.
The benches soon bore them, their battle-dress clattered,
330 Their spears were soon stacked, these seafarers' weapons,
Like a spinney of spears, splendid gray ash,
With the troop no less true, all tested in battle.
Then a proud noble probed, and put them a question.
He asked of their origins, his opinion not hidden.
"Whence have you wandered as warriors so fell
And brought all this battle-gear, this bounty of might,
These shields, these spears, these summons of death?
I am Hrothgar's herald and his high-retainer,
And never have known such nobility in wanderers.
340 Surely bravery or battle, not banishment, brings you
To Heorot and Hrothgar, to have such a presence."
Then man spoke to man, as majesty would have it,
The great Geat leader gave quick reply,
Hard in his helmet, "We are Hygelac's men,
My name, bestowed at birth, is Beowulf.
If that master of men, most famed of kings,
High over all, Halfdane's son, will hear me out,
I would be grateful to greet him and give him my errand,
Make known my mission, and make him aware."
350 Wulfgar then, prince of Wendels, warrior renowned,
With wisdom well known and a well-tempered spirit,
Said, "I will serve as your herald and seek out an answer,
From our devoted Dane-king, daring in battle,
That giver of gifts, that great giver of rings.
I will question the king, your quest announcing,
And bring back an answer to beckon you to him,
The audience your entrance has eagerly sought from him."
And the tall warrior, turning, past the tables he walked
To where Hrothgar held court, at the head of the hall.

Gray-bearded, grizzled, and grim in his majesty,
Solemn, surrounded by nobles, he served face to face.
Wulfgar spoke to his sovereign, standing fast in the courtesies.
"These men are a marvel, they made it from Geatland,
Sailing over seas to speak with you now.
Battle-hardened, brave, with Beowulf their leader,
Lord of the Shieldings, they seek to speak with you now.
They want to have words, they would have your ear.
My high lord Hrothgar, you hold their request,
So do not deny them, disappointment forestall.
These warriors are worthy, their weapons are noble,
Their bearing is brilliant, their bravery outstanding.
Mark their champion and chief who chose such retainers."

SEVENTH FITT † *Hrothgar and Beowulf meet, "Fate must go as it must"*

Hrothgar, Shield to the Shieldings, summoned reply:
"Why, I knew this young noble, and never forgot him.
His father, justly famous, was fated as Ecgtheow.
Hrethel the Geat gave him the gift of his daughter,
Such that their son is here seeking out friendship.
It is time to determine the tests of old loyalties.
Some men, of our merchants, made their way to the Geats,
To carry gifts for the giving, graven presents and thanks.
They were sent back with stories. The strength of thirty
They said was stored in the strength of his hand.
Now holy God in His goodness has guided him here,
In His manifest mercy, in His manifold kindness,
To desperate Danes to defend us from Grendel.
Send him in, send him in, summon him quickly,
I will truly offer treasures, for his tested courage.
I hope in his heroism, I will hand him great bounty.

Go now and get him and gather him quickly.
390 Bring him. Our barons will boast to have met him.
Greet them warmly and worthily, tell them welcome to Denmark."
Wulfgar went to the door, and welcomed them heartily.
"My lord, leader of Danes, your lineage knows
And says that your surety is strength in your battles.
He salutes your seafaring and summons your courage.
Come in, come in, and come in your armor,
Wearing helms to see Hrothgar, and Heorot bids welcome.
Your spears must be stacked, your shields must remain
Until kingly counsel has concluded this matter."
400 That hero, high-minded, held silent and rose,
With thanes powerful and potent, but part of them stayed
To watch the weapons as their warrior-chief directed.
Their prince led; they proceeded and passed through the door
Into Heorot's haven with a brave-helmet leading.
He strode forward and stood to speak with the king.
Then brave Beowulf spoke, bold in his armor,
Chested in chain-mail the chosen smith had woven—
"Hail to Hrothgar! May good health not leave you.
I am from Hygelac's hall, a strong help in his battles.
410 Many mighty young deeds my master received once.
Then news of Grendel to Geatland came, grim were the tidings.
Sailors told stories of your suffering people,
How this great and good hall lies ghostly and empty
To your warriors, once evening comes, once the sun has set
And the light lowers its way below the lip of the world.
All our elders advised me, our wise men gave counsel,
Saying I should sail, cross the sea to your service,
Offer help to you, Hrothgar, give help to the Danes.
They never had known a naked strength greater,
420 Had seen me bloodied by blows, but battling through it.

I beat down and bound some beasts, five in number,
I took out a troll-nest, I tackled sea monsters
On the water and waves, drove warriors from Geatland,
Who honestly asked for it. I was eager to do it.
Undaunted I drove them, devastating them quickly.
And so against Grendel I give out my challenge,
To settle that score in single combat.
So, Shield of the Shieldings, grant this single favor—
Having come this far, do not refuse me. My ferocity simmers,
Bold king of the Bright-Danes, their bravest defender.   430
Grant me this gift, ring-giver and king,
Grant me the pleasure to purify this palace called Heorot
With my men, masterful all, I mention no others.
I have heard this hard monster uses no help from weapons,
Reckless, scorns to submit to the swordplay we use.
To heighten Hygelac's glory, that his heart may be gladdened,
I renounce sword and shield and will serve you bare-handed.
I will waive this thick war-board and will wage hand to hand
My fight with that fiend and will finish his story,
Foe against foe, I will fight for us all.   440
Death comes, one will die, he will deem it God's justice,
Who settles and summons His servants inscrutably.
If this ghoul Grendel wins, he will gruesomely devour
The Geats in that grim hall, and will gobble them down
As he did, devouring, those dead in your war-hall.
My face won't be favored with a final death-covering,
He will carry me cold, no comfort will greet me,
As he, gorged and gloating, will run to ground to devour.
My body all bloodied will be battered and torn,
Will be food for that fiend as in a frenzy he eats me,   450
Fouling his fetid nest as my final chapter,
No laments, no long mourning, no lays to be sung,

No funeral is fitting, no final rites or observances.
But if battle bests me, Hrethel's brilliant war shirt
Should be reverently returned from this retainer to Hygelac—
Weland wove it. Wyrd[4] must go as it must.

EIGHTH FITT † *Hrothgar's speech and welcome*

Hrothgar, helm of the Shieldings, held forth as he spoke,
"Beowulf, brave friend, bringing the best of help,
Out of kindness you came, with the comfort of strength.
460 Your father once fought, and a great feud erupted
When he killed and conquered that capable Heatholaf,
A warrior among Wulfings, with his own hand.
The wantonness of war was wending its way,
And fearing, his folk shunned him, and forced him to leave.
Undaunted, he came to the Danes, and dwelt here with us.
He wrestled waves rolling, he witnessed our kindness
And the South-Danes served him as true sons of honor.
Unused to rule, I was a young king then, yearning to grow,
Establishing sway over strongholds, and settling the wealth.
470 Heorogar, son of Halfdane, did not hold to life.
Elder brother and better man, in battle he went down.
I sent wergild to the Wulfings, over the water I sent it,
And Ecgtheow acknowledged me and accepted strong oaths.
It burdens my breast to believe that I must
Reveal the wreckage that rivalry with Grendel has wrought,
What havoc, what humiliation, what hell he has brought us.
My ranks have been ravaged, my realm has been weakened,
Fate has not favored us, fighting is futile,
Swept by a strength that is stronger than all of us.
480 But God can take Grendel, and use a good man to do it.

---

4. *Wyrd* is the word we get *weird* from. Think of it as being in the grasp of an uncanny fate.

Time after time when the toping was strong,
Strong thanes thought to meet him and thickened in courage
Said they would slay him and summoned their ale-strength
To be heroes in Heorot, to be hailed in the mead-hall.
They sharpened their swords and silently waited.
But daybreak and dawn showed their dark blood on the floor,
Slick and sickening, blood spattered on benches,
My following faltered and feasting diminished.
Tested and tried we were all taught to fear.
Now sit to your supper and seek to untie your thoughts,   490
Great warrior, give to us, gifts as you desire."
Then a bench was brought, a bench was cleared
For the Geats to gather, together to sit down.
In courage they came quite proud in their bearing.
A servant was summoned and served out the mead-ale,
The gold pitcher was good, the good ale was brighter.
The scop would sing, his song filled the hall,
A herald of hope, and Heorot was glad.
The gathered men were glad, both Geat and Dane.

NINTH FITT † *Unferth and Beowulf clash*

Crouching by the king's stool was a crafty man,   500
Unferth, son of Ecglaf, undone by envy,
Carping, he spoke contrary to the coming of Beowulf—
Sea-bravery, strength in battle, sickened that man,
Who, vicious and vexed, had his vitals eaten by envy.
He would not grant greatness to other good men,
Under heaven he held that all honor was *his*.
"Beowulf? who challenged Breca in boats on the open sea?
That rowing test was risky, your rivalry great.
In pride you proceeded, you proved you were boastful,
Risking the deep, no restraint, if reckoned in pride.   510

Foe or friend, no facts could dissuade you,
Both of you boasting, your boats in the water,
Stroking, boats swimming, you slid from the bay,
Embracing water, eager, you entered that trial,
Manic and mulish, you measured the sea-roads,
Riding swells of the sea, which swayed like your pride.
The winter waves rose, and wild was the rowing.
You toiled in the tempest, you took seven nights,
Driven by desperate waves, the deep almost took you,
520   In that contest he conquered, came to shore victorious,
Washed to shore by the sea, safe near the Heathoreams.
He belonged to the Brondings, and back he returned,
To the place he preferred, becoming prince to his people.
So Breca, son of Beanstan, has bested you fully,
Fulfilling his future, your fears have been realized.
No matter your mettle has been measured in battle,
Your battles and bouts, your belligerence tested,
If you dare to defy him, this demon of Heorot,
You'll die to greet Grendel, this ghoul in the hall."
530   Ecgtheow's son answered, the utterance of Beowulf,
"Unferth, you utter mere words, Unferth my friend,
Your *beer* talks of Breca, it's beer wisdom I hear.
The truth is more telling, I can tell *that* adventure.
I had more strength for the stroke, though the seas were hard.
I held up under hardship, in high waves and water.
As boys like to boast—as boys we grew up—
We decided to do it, and we did as we said.
The ocean was open, open, inviting,
We dared to defy it, however daunting it was.
540   With swords to serve us, we shoved off from the beach.
The sea roiled, we rowed, with real steel to protect us
From whale-beasts in winter, from watery monsters.

Breca couldn't break from me, his back bent to the rowing,
Nor could I pull away past him, though powerfully stroking.
Shoulder to shoulder we struggled five nights
Until the deep drove us, divided us finally.
The wintery waves, the wicked cold drove us apart,
The perishing north wind, pointed, pounded us fiercely,
Dark night, deep waters, stirred the deep creatures,
Agitated and angered them, all of them wild.   550
My chain mail, chosen well, was choice for that battle,
Hand-forged, hard-linked, it held up against them.
A woven war-shirt, worked with gold,
Covered my courage, encasing my heart.
A sea-dragon dragged me down to the deep bottom,
Pinned and pinioned, my point finally reached him,
My sharp sword drove in, I stabbed as I could.
That battle-blow reached him, that sea beast was slain,
A huge, hungry monster my hand finally conquered.

TENTH FITT † *Sea creatures, Unferth silenced, vow to Wealhtheow*

"Again and again angry creatures rose up,   560
Lurking and lunging. I lashed with my sword,
My battle blade served me, I bested them all.
My sword-feast, their sorrow, they suffered my blows,
Dark things from the deep who would devour me happily
On the sunken seabed, savaging my bones.
In the morning these monsters, mangled and pierced,
Asleep from my sword, were softened and rotting,
So much dead debris, destined for nothing.
I brought safety for sailors, with those sea monsters dead.
Light lifted the east, light covered the land,   570
The bright beacon of God, a balm for the seas.

Then I saw sea-cliffs, the shore of the headlands,
Those windswept walls. Wyrd often delivers
The doughty and daring if dauntless he stands.
And so I now summon you to seek out such a tale,
When nine sea-beasts were nailed in fierce night battle,
Killed by my craft, killed dead with my sword.
Near death, desolate, on the deep I floated,
How I came unharmed from that hostile brood,
580 How I lived to see light the Lord only knows.
Though spent with the struggle, the sea brought me,
On the flood with the flotsam, to Finland's coast.
Now I don't hear such deeds being dealt out to Unferth,
Your boasts—and Breca's—have such battle not seen.
Your swords were not celebrated, not seen in such straits,
Or for facing such fights on the field of battle.
Not to boast of my battles, I bested my enemies.
But your kith and kin were killed by your hand,
Your closest kinsmen, the curse of Hell waits for you,
590 Corrupted by cruelty, however clever you are.
I tell you the truth, you true son of Ecglaf,
The grim deeds of Grendel would not have gotten this far,
That malicious monster, your master distressing,
Wrecking havoc in Heorot, if your heart for battle
Were as bold as your boasts, that beast would be dead.
But he finds no feud from you, no fierce rush of swords,
No dread of the Danes, no death from your weapons.
He vaunts over Victor-Shieldings, his vicious glee
Takes his tribute, he tastes his spoils
600 In the land of lost Danes, in his lust for the kill,
He kills, he consumes, no counterattacks
From stalwart Spear-Danes, no strength in response.
But I will soon show him what strength is made for,

The pride and power of Geats will prove the point to him.
After battle, brave to mead, the best may go,
When the sun rises soon on the sons of men,
And the light lifts his face to lighten our way."
The treasure-giver took hope, he tasted it now,
White-bearded, war-brave, he had waited long.
That Bright-Danes' best prince from Beowulf heard   610
The first hope, firm hope, and with fisted resolve.
Then loud laughter came from liegemen rejoicing
With words that were winsome. Then Wealhtheow entered,
Hrothgar's high queen, heeding all courtesies,
Greeting these guests, gold-arrayed and lovely,
That high-hearted lady handed the first cup,
To the conquering Dane-king, the cup filled to the rim.
She bade him the best; the beer was golden.
He was lauded and loved in the lives of his people,
So gladly she gave it, he gladly received it.   620
The Helmings' high queen in the hall walked regally,
Carrying the cup, that queen was their servant,
Offering up mead to all elders and youths,
Till that royal-ringed woman, rich beyond measure,
Came to brave Beowulf with the beer in her hand,
And greeted the Geat lord, and gave thanks to God,
Speaking wise words. Her wish was fulfilled
Through a hero to hope in, through a hero in truth,
Who came bringing comfort. The cup he received,
That warrior was welcomed by Wealhtheow's hand.   630
He spoke serenely, though seeking out combat.
Then Beowulf spoke brave words, the best son of Ecgtheow,
"My thanes and I thought on the thickness of battle
When we entered the ship and embarked to the ocean.
To fight to the finish, or fail the attempt,

Was the work we wanted, and the will of your nation.
So I am firm for this fight, and the fiend's grip will take me,
Or I will take him and test him, or my tale ends here.
That woman was well-pleased having witnessed his valor,
640 This battle-heart of Beowulf, this boast of a good man.
Bright in gold, beautiful, emboldened she sat
By Hrothgar her husband, in the hall both presiding.
As before, brave words spoken with bustle and chatter,
Warriors' great words wafted upwards like smoke,
A confident company till it came time for bed.
Hrothgar, son of Halfdane, was heedful of rest,
For he knew that the night would bring nothing but battle,
A fight with a fiend in the festival hall,
When the great shining sun was seen no longer,
650 And the darkness, deep darkness, brought the demon to haunt them,
And shadowy shapes came slinking around.
The warriors, all weary, rose well-ready for bed,
Both leaders took leave, good luck for the moment,
Hrothgar held out his hand, and hailed the young warrior,
Gave him the hall, the wine-hall to guard it.
"Since shouldering my shield, since sheltering my people,
Never before have I bound the hall over
To the hand and the heart of another high warrior,
Except now to such a great servant as you.
660 Recall and remember resplendent glory,
So watch for that wicked one, no wish will fail you
If you conquer and kill him, if you come through alive."

ELEVENTH FITT † *Asleep in Heorot, Beowulf trusts God*

Hrothgar, hero-king, and his house-guard departed.
Shielding king, shelter of the people, sought his rest

With his best bed-comfort, his bride-queen, Wealhtheow.
The conflict was coming but the King-of-Glory
Had set a guard against Grendel, that grim marauder,
So men heard the heroics of the hall-defender,
Who guarded the great king, with good intent.
In truth he trusted the tested strength of his arm   670
And in the goodness and greatness of God over all.
He took off his tunic, his trusted iron corselet,
His head unhelmeted, he handed his sword
To his selected steward—that sword was the finest—
Told him to guard the gear, the gear from his battles.
Then Beowulf, before they bedded down
Gave out a great boast, good although proud,
"In a fight I hold fast, no feebler I am,
Than Grendel the grim would grant for himself.
And so with the sword I do not seek to fight   680
But his life I will lift from him, *that* lies in my power.
He knows nothing of war-craft, no knowledge of the arts,
No shield work or sword play, though his strength is great.
We both are bold, so in battle tonight
We shall spurn sword work, if he seeks me here,
With no weapons for this warfare. Let only wise God,
Our living Lord, lift His countenance on one
And decree the doom of it as He deems right."
The chief reclined, and rested, his right cheek on the pillow,
His noble head nodded, night came,   690
His sea-roving sailors sank to rest on their beds.
None thought that survival—night thickened with danger,
From hall-floor to home, thoughts hurrying on
To the land they loved—would lead them back!
Full well they knew warriors were wasted by Grendel,
Death seized many Danes in the dreaded hall,

But conquest and comfort were coming to them—
God's war-loom was weaving to the Weders this victory.
He gave greatness to one, a grip of deliverance,
700 A single man's strength to save all the people.
The truth can be told now, this tale of deliverance:
The Most High, His majesty weaves marvels for men.
He always rules over men, in Almighty wisdom.
Then down through the darkness the demon approached,
The shadow-stalker came, stealthy and vile.
The guards were slack, sleeping, silent, unconscious.
All but one, Beowulf, that brave deliverer, who knew
Into darkness the demon could not drag any man
Apart from the providence of the perfect God.
710 One man was masterful, a mind filled with battle.

TWELFTH FITT † *Grendel is disturbed and advances*

Out of the marsh, by misty crags, the marauder crept.
Grendel, under God's wrath, came greedy for blood.
The bane of brave warriors, emboldened and turning
Toward the high hall, hungry for flesh.
Under mist, in the murk, till the mead-hall he spied,
He came in his cruelty—the hall crafted in gold,
Weary yet wonderful, a witness to joy.
This, Hrothgar's home, a haven for nobles,
He had battered before, but his bane waited now.
720 The hall held great heroes and hard luck for Grendel.
Lost and alone, that lost soul kept coming,
He crept as he came, and crushed the great doorway,
With fisted, great fury, and fire in his stomach,
Boiling in blood-lust, he burst out in anger.
Door hinges were hanging, he hastily entered.

The bright-patterned pavers he polluted by walking,
He stood, then he strode, anger streamed from his eyes,
Flamed, then flashed, like fire it was.
In the hall heroes slept, he hungered to see them,
Kinsmen and clansmen all clustered and sleeping,   730
Lieutenants and liegemen. He laughed in his malice,
For the monster had mind, before morning could come,
To savage each soul, to sink his teeth into them,
Greedy and gluttonous, Grendel was ravenous,
And wanted his way, but wyrd put a stop to it.
Never after that night would he knead a man's bones.
Watching and waiting, the warrior from Hygelac
Watched the cursed killer and counted the seconds.
How the monster would move, making his play—
Not that the were-shape would wait very long!   740
Straightway he seized a slumbering warrior,
His first prey, and fiercely he fisted the carcass,
Bit him down to the bone, his blood he drank greedily,
He grabbed him in gobs, and gobbled him down.
In one moment the monster had mashed and devoured him,
Both feet and both hands, and blood on the floor.
He walked toward our warrior, to welcome the second,
Extending his talon to take up another,
But Beowulf, boldly, bested his reach,
Propped up and powerful, prompt in response.   750
Then that sin-shepherd soon saw far more trouble
Than he ever encountered in all middle-earth,
In marshes, on moors, the might of such strength,
Such a heavy, hard hand-grip, his heart started quailing,
Perturbed and then panicked, powerless to flee.
He recoiled, retreating, he wanted to run off to
His devil den. This dealing was new,

He never had known such knocks in the old days.
Then brave Beowulf, his boast fresh remembered,
760   Surged in his strength and strained all he had,
He grasped his foe firmly, whose fingers were cracking,
The giant got off, the great man soon followed him.
With eagerness eating him, the monster intended
To flee, to get free, and to fly far away,
To take flight to his fens, his fingers were slipping
In the grip of that grim one. No good was this trip
To the great hall of Heorot, no happiness *here*.
Timbers rocked and the racket revealed the great tumult,
The Danes heard the din, and the daring could listen
770   To the ultimate beer brawl, that battle careened
From wall to wall—wonderfully the hall stood.
The fighters were furious and fought all in,
The timbers shook, but stood, the struggle continued,
The strain of that struggle, sustained, taut,
Threatened the thick beams but throughout it stood,
Held within and without by wide iron bands,
Cunningly crafted, but they continued crashing
Through many mead-benches—men still talk of it—
Glistering with gold, for all the grim foes cared,
780   The way they wracked it. The wisest Shieldings never thought
That any man or ogre strong or eager warrior,
Could hurt or harm that horn-tipped hall—
Only torching fire could touch it, only terror hot
With scorching smoke could soon bring it down.
A roar redoubled, and redoubtable Danes
With fear were filled, with frenzied panic,
Standing guard at the garrison, hearing Grendel's howl.
That hellish howl was heard by everyone,
The cry of that captive, his clamor and pain

Was heard down in Hell. Beowulf held him,
Stalwart, stubborn, the strongest of men
Who ever earned honor under the sun.

Thirteenth Fitt † *Fight with Grendel*

That earl-warrior was eager to see emptiness take him,
To catch this night-caller—this killer must die,
His life was no loss, his liberty shaken
By a mighty man. Now many Geats
Flailed in fury with their finest swords,
Protecting their prince, their power tremendous,
But all of their blows bounced off his hide.
They had not known, nearing their enemy,
These hardy friends, heroes, these high-hearted warriors,
Swinging their swords from several sides,
That the keenest blade could not kill the creature.
The best blade on earth would bounce off harmlessly,
Not hurting or harming that hideous beast.
Safe under spells, from swords and from weapons,
From edged wrath and iron. Yet his end was upon him,
His life was soon leaving, his lights were flickering,
His passing was painful, his passion was agony,
His descent to the devil was discovered as loathsome.
He who had harried men and hated their joys,
Hostile to holiness, his heart feuding with God,
He had murdered many and men greatly feared him,
But his frame failed him, this fiend lost his grip.
Hygelac's hero, that high-hearted warrior,
Held death in his hand grip, his hold was tremendous.
Each one of them hated that the other one lived.
That creature then cracked, his cruelty rewarded,

His broad shoulder burst, and bloody sinews popped,
820 Those bones were broken. To Beowulf belonged
The glory that was given, and Grendel was driven
To his den, to his death, in the dark marshes waiting,
In the fens' filthiness he was fleeing in sorrow
To the end of his ugliness, to the end of his life.
The desire of the Danes, their dearest wishes,
Were fulfilled in fierce battle, by the finest of warriors.
Their rescue from ravages was wrested in freedom
For Hrothgar's hall. The heroic wise warrior
Had purged its pollutions. He was pleased by his work,
830 His devotion and deed. To the Danes of the east
His boast was believed, his bravery delivered
Them from sadness and sorrows, their sickness in envy,
The bane of this battle they had borne for too long,
The pain and pollution, the passions of hatred.
The proof of proud victory, presented in gladness,
When the hard warrior's hand held the grim trophy,
The talon he tore off, with the torn arm and shoulder,
And Grendel's long grip to the gable was nailed.

FOURTEENTH FITT † *Giddy retainers, story of Heremod*

Many came in the morning, this marvel to see,
840 Gathering at the gift-hall to gawk at the trophy,
Clan chiefs coming, compassing great distances,
Along wide, wandering roads, in their wonder discussing
The monster's fell footprints. His fatal departure
Did not give them grief, that grim flight recorded
By the trail of tracks, and the tale it told.
Despairing, the demon had disappeared,
Wracked and ruined, to the wretched monster lake,

Doomed and despairing, he dragged bloody footprints.
The blood boiled in the water, bucking and seething,
Swirls of hot wound-slurry,[5] surging in turmoil,   850
Oozing out envy and utter disaster.
Facing his death-fate, his fen then received him,
Lurking, and luckless, from life he relinquished
His hard-hearted soul. Hell came then and took him.
Spirits high, singing, old soldiers and young ones,
Rode home on horseback, hailing the hero.
Beowulf's brave deed was blessed and applauded,
By well-mounted men, by men beyond joyful.
They praised and praised more, they persisted in saying
That far north or near south, between nether seas,   860
In the whole world, no warrior was better;
Under heaven's high sky, no heroic shield-bearer,
Would ever win more and be more worthy of rule.
But they laid no blame on their lord, they left him alone,
Hrothgar was held blameless. What a *good* king that was!
At times the good men galloped, their gray horses racing,
Released and running when the road was straight,
And the path and the place were perfectly well-known.
And song after song the scop would recount
From his storehouse of stories, singing with wisdom,   870
Glorying in good words, the great, ancient tales.
One after another he eagerly sang them,
Weaving in wisdom, old words with new ones,
Praising Beowulf's power, and proving his talent,
With a lay and well-fashioned lines, that lifted up fame.
Braiding his best words with the best deeds of men.
He sang of the strength of Sigemund's arm,

---

5. This magnificent kenning is Seamus Heaney's.

His fame and his feats, and fearsome marvels,
The wandering of Wael's son—the wide roads he traveled,
880 The foul deeds and feuds, and fighting unknown
Except to Fitela, his friend, who would never forsake him.
When he desired to discuss these deeds with somebody,
They were nephew and near-uncle, they both knew the stories,
As battle-friends, brave together, they brought enemies down.
Conquering they killed a whole clan of giants,
Seeking with swords to signal their glory.
After the day he died, undimmed was his glory,
Because Sigemund had slaughtered the serpent, that dragon,
That taker of treasure, that taster of gold.
890 That great prince under graystone gave the dragon the point,
Daring and dauntless, and doing it alone,
He saw the grim serpent, and his sword went home
Through the shining scales of the serpent and dragon,
Who was pierced with the point and pinned to the wall,
That dragon died. The daring of his slayer
Meant he had mounds of magnificent treasure.
The son of Wael wasted no time, weighed down his boat,
All the hold could hold, and it held a great deal.
He carried dazzling treasures down, before the dragon then melted.
900 He was famed as a fighter, his ferocity unmatched,
A baron of battle, the best in the business,
His great and good deeds, all gained by his courage.
King Heremod's health faltered, his hard campaigning slowed,
His valor was vanquished, victory lost to the giants.
Betrayed by black moods, backed into a corner,
He met death, deserted, deserving no better.
His sickness and sorrow had sunk his people,
With despair, disappointment, and death for his nobles.
Experienced men damned that expedition in those earlier times,

Who knew that nobility should not bring affliction
From haughtiness, hubris, and hollow arrogance.
They proposed that a prince should protect the people,
Prosper the people and nation, and preserve them from danger,
Taking title and treasure, but not to torment them,
That homeland of heroes, the home of the Shieldings.
Beowulf was better, and believed to be better,
Heremod was harried, hollowed out by sin.
Still racing, rejoicing, the retainers paced their horses,
On the sandy and single road that sent them all homeward.
Well after daybreak, delighted, doughty warriors
Gathered to the gift-hall to see the great marvel.
The king himself came from the queen's quarters,
Regal and royal, the ring-treasure guardian,
Well-known and noble, knights and earls with him,
A column of comfort, the queen right beside him,
And beautiful, bountiful, a bevy of women.

FIFTEENTH FITT † *Hrothgar views arm, Beowulf wishes he had corpse*

Hrothgar held forth, on the hall's steps he stood,
Under steep eaves, standing, sure-footed, regal,
With the roof garnished in gold, and Grendel's great claw.
"For this fine sight—finally!—I cannot fail to thank
Sovereign God with submission. Our sorrows were plenty,
Both raids and wrath, and ruin from Grendel, but
God gives wonder after wonder, the wise herder of glory.
Not long ago I had lost any lively hope,
Weighted with woes and wasted in grief.
I thought as long as I lived I would be lost in this misery,
With blood staining the stones of this stately great house.
Wise men withered in counsel, the woe had no relief,

We had no hope of hindering this hellish marauder—
940 Infernal foes and fiends found their way nightly,
Harrowing our hall. Through this hero now,
By the wisdom and work of God, this wonder is done,
Which all of our wisdom would not work for us.
For Beowulf's bravery, blessed among women
Is she who bore this bairn, who brought us our freedom.
To the sons of men I say, if she still lives,
That the God of all goodness was great through her.
Now, Beowulf, best of men, in battle triumphant,
As a son I laud and love you, lift your name high,
950 Keep this new kinship, carry it with you,
Acknowledge and nurture it, know that it's yours.
All worldly wealth here I would gladly give to you.
For lesser victories, lesser men, largess has been given
From my hoard in this hall to honor lesser achievements,
By men less stout and steadfast. You surpass them,
Fulfilling your fame in all future ages,
Your name will be known and nobility remembered,
If the God of goodness gives recognition to you."
So Beowulf, son of Ecgtheow, spoke in response,
960 "This was a willing war, a work that I sought out.
I have fought the good fight, and faced down this devil.
But I wished for a greater win, with Grendel whipped and dead,
Lying defeated and dead, devastated on this floor.
My strategy had been to seize, and in my strength to pin him down,
To grapple that grim demon, and with my grip to kill him.
I planned to pin him down, powerless, holding him,
Until that brute should stop breathing—but he broke free.
I could not keep him—the Creator did not will it—
His panicked hatred I could not hinder, and he hid deep in the night,
970 My lock on his life slipped, but he left a token behind!

He ran and in running vain rescue he sought.
He left his curdled cruelty, his claw and shouldered arm,
Left behind, bleeding; my boast is nailed there.
That wicked wretch ran wailing off
And won't live long, that loathsome criminal,
Sunken in sin, with sorrow astride him,
Death's grip has grasped him, he has been grabbed by anguish,
Though sadly my grip slipped, I say Death's will not,
Guilt dripping, blood drying, his doom approaching,
Whatever Majestic Wisdom means, whatever the Maker doles out." 980
The son of Ecglaf was silent then, his speech was stopped,
All his boastful words of bravery, his battle-prowess talk,
Since the nobles all had noted not one of them was greater
Than that hideous hand on the high eaves nailed,
Gigantic fingers grim, those gray-clawed spikes,
Like burnished steel, bent spikes, short spears for infighting,
Savage, wicked sharp, and seething with rage
Though dead, still deadly, though done with fighting,
That uncanny claw terrified. It was clear to all of them
That no man's blade or bravery could battle through that hide, 990
However sharp, no sword could sever that thing,
That bloody battle-claw from that beast full of hatred.

SIXTEENTH FITT † *Heorot refurbished*

The command soon came to reconstruct the hall,
And all hands were assembled, and all pitched in with a will.
Wise men and women the wine-hall restored.
The tales found in tapestries were told from the walls
With golden good woven in, and the guest-rooms refurbished,
The splendor was shining again, the scene magnificent.
Though braced with bands of iron, though bolstered with metalwork,

1000 The building was broken, battered and ruined,
Hinges were hanging loose; the hall roof alone
Was sound and safe, unscathed by that monster's flight,
When bloody and beaten, he fell back in his panic,
Despairing and dying, his destiny chasing.
No man runs from *that* ruin—realize that now.
Each soul, all souls, every one taking breath
Must make our way to the maw of death,
All men, sons of middle-earth, must make our solemn way.
Our bodies on beds of death, after the banqueting of life,
1010 To that destiny come in death, which deals the final blow.
The hour came for Halfdane's son, and the hall received him,
For the king came in and called them all to feast.
I have never heard such a host in happier noise,
No group more graciously gathered around a giver of rings.
The benches were bowed under the battle-warriors' weight,
Round after round of the royal mead passed.
The mead-cups were many, and mighty men drank them.
Hrothgar and Hrothulf were in high spirits,
Powerful kinsmen came together, close in friendship.
1020 Heorot was full of friends, at least full for the present.
Betrayal and treachery were untested as yet.
Then Halfdane's stalwart son gave a standard to Beowulf,
A gift fashioned from gold, a guidon of victory,
An embroidered battle pennant, a breastplate, a helmet,
And a splendid sword which many saw presented.
It was borne to Beowulf, and best honored that triumph.
He gracefully received the gifts, and good they were,
And Beowulf drank deeply there, no dishonor was present.
I have not heard of any heroes so honored,
1030 With fantastic gifts, cunningly fashioned, and *four* of them,
Silvered mead-bench ceremony, solemn and glad.

On the raised ridge of the helmet, the red was prominent,
Wound tight with wires, and was warden and sentry,
Lest an assault from a sword should strike the wearer,
And it go sharp in the strife when with shield he went forth
To fight with his foes and find them in battle.
Then the king commanded a cluster of horses be brought,
Eight of them in all, embroidered with bridle gold,
Their handlers came into the hall—one horse decked out
With a saddle set with jewels, studded, resplendent;   1040
It had been Hrothgar's when high-hearted to battle
He used to go to adventure when eager swords clashed.
His courage in combat never cowered or quailed;
He was daring and doughty when dead bodies fell.
The honorable Ingwine king gave authority to Beowulf
Over these weapons and war-horses, wished him wise in their use,
Bidding him steward his bravery, the best way in fighting.
So the Danes' leader and lord led them in gratitude,
Dispensed from his hoard to the hero, and handsomely paid him
With horses, high treasure, and humble acknowledgement   1050
As those who love this tale will tell—the truth is obvious.

SEVENTEENTH FITT † *Beowulf rewarded, "Lay of Finn" begins*

The king then came, as custom decreed,
Gave the companions who crossed the cresting seas with Beowulf
Great heirlooms, good honors—gifts to the ale-bench with him,
Precious and priceless gifts; he paid the penalty, the wergild,[6]
In gold for the one Grendel ate, that grim repast,
A foul murder; many more would have met death

---

6. A *wergild* is a ransom payment to fend off vengeance. Hrothgar had paid the wergild for
Beowulf's father earlier, and he is paying it again now—assuming that since Grendel, their
monster, had killed one of the Geats, they might have sought vengeance against the Danes.

Had not the wisdom of wise God their wyrd deflected
Through that brave man's mettle. The Maker and Creator
1060 Rules mankind by measure, and means it for good.
Therefore, think ahead always, thoughtful preparation is best,
Forethought and foresight forestall worry of mind.
Since woe and weal fill this world of troubles,
Through the length of life's battles, which linger long enough.
Then melodic music mingled in the rafters,
When for Halfdane's heir the harpist played,
Stroking the strings and singing a lay.
The bard woke battle-joy in the mead benches' fighters
With a stirring song of the sudden raid
1070 And assault on the settlements of the sons of Finn.
Halfdane's great hero, Hnaef the Shielding,
Was to fall stricken, fated, in that Frisian combat.
High-hearted Hildeburh did not hold in honor
The Jutes and their jealousy. Judge her innocent—
She lost loved ones, and lost on both sides,
Her grown boy and brother, they both suffered death,
Struck by spears—her sorrow was deep.
Keening, not without cause, she kept up her lament.
None doubted Hoc's daughter saw the dawn's bloody greeting,
1080 When under the unforgiving sky she understood death,
Murder claimed her kinsmen, and kept her in sorrow,
All her peace and pleasant things passed from the world.
Just a few followers with Finn were left,
And he could not conquer or quell Hengest's men,
Those warriors with weapons, so more war was fruitless,
His remnant unrescued by his right arm.
A pact of peace he offered, parleyed to terms—
The Danes could dwell there, done with fighting,
Sharing high-seat and hall and half authority,

Joined with the Jutes, and justice agreed upon, 1090
Shared giving of goods and gladness together.
Folcwada's son saluted and summoned great gifts,
Favored Hengest's folk with fabulous rings,
True treasure given, and torques bejeweled,
And splendid gold, and silver, stores of wealth.
To spur the fealty of Frisians was first in his mind,
His own tribe, as tales say, as told in the alehouse.
So the pact of peace produced the strongest bonds,
Firmly held a final peace. Finn to Hengest
With oath upon oath and honor committed, 1100
So the wretched remnant would reckon it wise
To be nobly ruled, no hatreds, so none of these men
By word waken trouble or work their resentments,
Or in malice of mind mention their grief
In forgetting the feud that felled their chieftain,
Lost, rudderless, leaderless, that lot was their fate.
But if some Frisian foe fought with taunting words,
To call back the cruelty, then come what may,
A sword must settle the summoned doom coming.
Oaths were enacted, and ancient treasures 1110
Were brought from burial places and bound the vows.
The great Shielding, good warrior, was given to the pyre.
That pyre was placed well, and plain to see,
With gilded boar, battle helmet, and bloody mail shirt,
And hard high-hearted warriors, all held by death,
Slain in the slaughter, with the sword cut down.
Hildeburh wailed for Hnaef, and her son as well,
Bidding his body be brought alongside,
That his bones might burn, and his body ascend,
Alongside his uncle, to the unfeeling sky. 1120
Her grief song was great, grim wailing ascended,

With the smoke of the slain and the songs of death mingling.
The fire was fierce, the fallen consumed,
Brains boiling over, blood gushing from wounds,
The bodies were bursting, the burning greedily ate
And gone were their great ones, their glory vanished.

Eighteenth Fitt † *Hengest plots revenge, Wealhtheow plans*

Those heroes were homesick, and hungered for Friesland,
Their friends were fallen and families far off,
Their homes and hearths were havens long missing.
1130 Hengest held on through the hard and long winter,
Keeping a prisoners' pact, and powerless to sail,
To point his curved prow to the pleasures of home,
Over wintery waves. Those waters were rough,
Either lashed by long storms or locked up in ice.
He sojourned there, simmering, waited springtime's arrival,
Bringing welcoming warmth to the waiting of men,
With the sun in the sky, the long season over.
The fields were fair, and full was the spring;
The guest of Finn gathered that good was the time
1140 To sail, but silent in thought, he sought first his vengeance,
Which his passion preferred to plowing the seas;
Wanting his hatred to hasten in the heat of his vengeance,
Wheeling his wrath on the unwitting Jutes.
And so the time for treachery tempted by rising,
When the high sword Hunlafing was held in his hand,
The brightest of blades was brought to his lap.
Feared by the Frisians, its fine edge was known.
He struck Finn, slaughtered him, stabbing him through,
Under his own roof, an ugly sword death.
1150 For Guthlaf and great Oslaf the grim attack had told

In sorrow and sadness after sea voyaging,
Lamenting their losses and losing their joy.
The wretched hall floor reddened and reeked with blood.
Finn was killed, cut down, his companions slaughtered,
Clansmen and king all; his queen was seized.
She was borne to their ship, the Shieldings took her,
With the chieftain's chattel, they chose their plunder.
They found and fingered all of Finn's treasures,
Whether gems or jewels or just the gold.
With the fabled fair queen a fair breeze then took them   1160
Over the deeps to Daneland, her despair going with them.
The lay and lament finished, and loud feasting resumed.
Bright clamor commenced, and cupbearers hustled
With wine in white flagons. Wealhtheow then rose,
To go in her gold crown where two good men were sitting,
An uncle and unfailing nephew, each one true to the other,
Persistent in peace. Pale Unferth was spokesman,
Sitting at the Shielding's feet, his spirit was known,
His courage unquestioned, though his kinsmen had felt
The force of his ferocity when fighting broke out.   1170
The queen said to the king, "This cup is yours,
Great-souled giver of rings, so good in your kindness,
Giver of gold to men; to the Geats now speak
Such kind words of comfort that kings should use.
Be generous to the Geats, bestow gifts that are worthy,
Recall what came to you, when kind gifts came your way.
I have heard it said in the hall that you hold this warrior
In esteem as an heir. This eager one purged Heorot,
Bright bejeweled ring-hall, the best of all halls,
So consider while you can how to come with great gifts   1180
To please your people before passing on
To greet your great judge. For gracious I think

My Hrothulf, high-hearted, to hold rule is ready
Over young noblemen now, if that long night you enter
Before him, high prince of Shieldings, hailing farewell to us.
I consider him kind and I call him to mind
To patiently repay these parents and their sons
For their honor and help that they held out for him,
Their gracious gifts and their giving of honor!"
1190 Then she came to the seat where her sons were seated,
Hrethric and Hrothmund with high honor seated,
With good and great noblemen, the Geat was there too,
Brave Beowulf between the two brothers.

NINETEENTH FITT † *Gifts bestowed on Beowulf*

She carried a cup to him, with kindness greeted him,
With gold-wire winding and words that were winsome.
She offered intertwined bands, two torques for his arms,
A mail shirt, magnificent rings, an immense collar of gold,
Larger than any left these days, no man alive has seen greater.
Such treasures were taken up and talked about since—
1200 I have never heard of such a hoard since Hama carried off
To his shining city that solid Brosing necklace,
Encrusted with custom jewels—now encrusted with hate,
Earning from Eormenric only enmity and spite—
But worth it in worldly terms. The Weder Hygelac,
Son of Swerting's son, had that shining necklace with him,
Under his banner, in battle, his booty defending.
But fickle is war, and wasteful, and so wyrd overwhelmed him,
That time when he taunted the terrors of war,
To fight with the Frisians. Fair ornaments and jewels
1210 He carried, costly gems, over the curling waves,
Tempting fate, testing wyrd, he tried death in his armor.

That king fell to the Franks, fatal the battle,
They took that torque, his trappings and chain mail,
The weaker warriors the warfare carried,
From the blast of battle, that bane of Hygelac,
And held the fatal field. The festivities resumed.
Wealhtheow said to the warriors, "Wear this well—
This treasured torque, please take it with our thanks,
And this breastplate, Beowulf, well-beloved friend.
May you prosper in privilege, and profit in life! 1220
May your strength be savored, but to these striplings here,
Kind counsel that carries them. I am concerned to repay you.
You have done such deeds that in days and years coming
Your fame will flourish, forever your honor will stand,
As far as circling seas, and the surge against the cliffs
And the headlands holding them. May you hold your honor well,
O prince, may you prosper with this pile of treasure,
Live blessed and beloved. To these bairns of mine
Show compassion, kindness, and concern for their gladness.
Here everyone to all others is only and ever true, 1230
Mild in manner, to their master they are loyal.
The thanes are all thoughtful, the throng is compliant,
Beer-flushed and brave, their boast is obedience."
Then she went to her seat. The splendor of feasting was great;
The warriors had much wine. Wyrd was not yet with them,
Although many of those men would their mortality own
After nightfall, never waking, and never see sun again.
Hrothgar stood high, and home to bed he went,
Countless men, careful to guard, were quiet and vigilant
In the royal hall, their resting place, they rolled their bedding 1240
Between the benches, set bolsters and pillows.
One beer-man in the banquet hall, no less brave than the others,
Under his doom and his danger went to death in that sleeping.

They were buttressed by bucklers by their beds, at the head,
And their bright body armor; on each bench there was set
In plain sight, polished, their proud battle-helmets,
Their spears, their shining mail, their swords at the ready.
Ready for combat, as custom decreed, they came to their rest
Ready for battle, ready for war, not relinquishing care,
1250 Whether home by the hearth, or harrying the foe
As wandering warriors, as wyrd would have it.
They stood to serve their king—they were solid men.

TWENTIETH FITT † *Grendel's mother kills in Heorot*

They all sank into sleep. But sorrow was stalking
The sleep of one soldier—as so often happened
When Grendel guarded that gold hall at night,
An evil ogre, until his doom fell on him,
His payback and penalty. It was plain at dawn
That a surviving avenger killed the vicious ghoul,
And the word was worthy and wise the report.
1260 Grendel's mother, grim beast, a ghastly dame,
A mother and monster, mourned her loss.
In the dread water, wet doom, she dwelt for centuries,
In the cold depths of cruelty, since Cain's time,
When he slew with a sword his sole brother,
Surviving his father's other son: spurned he fled,
A marked man with murder on his forehead,
He wasted in the wilderness. There went out from him
Such ghouls and grim beasts as Grendel, who preyed
On human flesh and human souls, and at Heorot found
1270 A waiting warrior watching for a fight,
The monster sought to maul, with his mighty strength he seized,
But that man remembered his might and his grip,

The great gift that God had given him.
He trusted in the true God, and took the mercies of God
As comfort and courage, and conquered his foe.
That fiend then failed, and fled the hall maimed,
Wretched, he ran to the realms of death,
That enemy of men. But his mother now,
Hungry and grim, would go on a rampage
Of grief and grim hate, eager to avenge her son.   1280
Up to the hall of Heorot where high-hearted Danes
Were sleeping, secure, and soon she burst in,
Turning the tables, a terror in the night,
That monster's mother. A measure less, though,
Was her terror told as in the tale of battle women,
Amazons, women in mail, than of men in arms,
When, hilt in hand, the hammer-edge swords
Cut through the crests of curious boar helms,
Blades wet with blood, and battle-tested.
Hard blades in the hall in every hand were gripped,   1290
Swords and spears at the ready, shields lifted,
Tight and tough they stood, no time for helmets
Or woven-chain warrior shirts when they woke to assault.
When that demonic dam was discovered she fled
To save her sorry life when seen by the thanes.
She caught up a companion, in cruelty and malice,
And fled toward her fen, firmly clutching her victim.
For high-hearted Hrothgar he was held as the dearest,
The finest of fighters, with fame across seas,
Whom she slew as he slept, a slumbering hero.   1300
Brave Beowulf was absent, his bedding and housing
Were held in a house with highest of honors,
After the gold was gifted to the Geat for his prowess.
Heorot was in high uproar; the hand-claw she recognized,

Blood-covered, bone out, and she bore it off.

Grief in the hall was great and no good was that transfer
Where the good king and the Geat had to give up bitterly
The lives of dear loved ones. The lord of the Danes,
The great, gray hero, with gravid soul
1310 Saw his soldier gone, slaughtered in malice,
Departed and dead, and a desolate king behind.
Beowulf was brought, beckoned in haste,
His deeds not yet done. As daylight spread,
He came with companions, a company of earls,
Where the wise king waited, worrying of fortune,
Wanting the World-Ruler to wield a better turn,
To take this miserable tale and turn it to good.
He strode over stone pavers, to the sovereign Beowulf came,
With his hearty and hale companions—the hall's floors echoed—
1320 Coming to greet the gracious king with goodly words,
Asking the dear lord of Danes if the dark has passed well,
If slumber was sweet and a salve to his mind.

TWENTY-FIRST FITT † *Hrothgar despairs and talks*

High-hearted Hrothgar spoke, helmet of the Shielding,
"Don't ask of delight, our doom has returned,
The dread of the Danes, and death to Aeschere,
Whose younger brother was Yrmenlaf . . . yesterday.
My rune-reader, my reliable adviser and sage,
A shield at my shoulder in the slashing of battle,
When warriors fought and we warded off blows,
1330 Our boar-crests bashed others, and battle was hot.
I wish all my earls were as Aeschere was.
But in Heorot an evil hand hated and murdered him,
A ghastly and ghoulish monster grabbed and took off,

She pounced, proud, and pursued her escape,
Full of her feud-lust, filled up with vengeance
For the death that you dealt and did it in strength,
When in your grasp, Grendel gave up on life.
You knew the night terrors, you knew how my thanes
Had been ravaged and wrecked. But ruined and conquered,
He fell before you. Now fatal cruelty comes,   1340
With fury and ferocity the feud to continue,
Seeking revenge, seething, settled on blood.
These thanes will think in deep thickness of grief
Their ring-giver is gone, a good man is dead.
This is hard on our hearts. A hand lies in death
That once won these men with willing gifts.
Land-holders and lieutenants who live in these parts,
Say they have seen several of these things,
A pair that imperils any poor souls out on the moor,
Border-stalkers, black strength, and born for haunting,   1350
Wandering wights, wailing ghouls,
And from the tales told one taller, one less,
One wraith a woman, the other wicked, accursed,
In man-shape, a monster, across marshes and meres
He slipped quietly, silent, skulking through bogs,
Larger in life than men, through long ages this Grendel,
Rural folk named and feared him, his father unknown.
His line was woven in wickedness, among wolves and ghosts
And demons and devils, desolate was their home.
They wandered cruel crags and cliffs at the headlands,   1360
Fetid fens, and foul the streams
Which cold from the cliffs came down through the rocks,
Choosing underground chambers. The choice is plain—
Not many miles from here the mere spreads out,
And the edge of the frost-bound forest fans out over black water,

The roots are rugged, and wrestle the shore.
On clear nights uncanny sights go cold to the bone,
The water burns and blazes, that bog smokes.
Our people have not plumbed the perils of that deep.
1370 Desperate, chased by dogs, a deer will stop short,
Rather than run on, he reels and turns,
Surrenders his soul, stopping to die,
He gasps and gives up, than to go in that lake.
That gulf is no good—"*Godforsaken.*"
When the wind works up, the waves arc and toss,
The clouds stream and scud when storms brew,
And that filth sags and surges and soon enough,
The holy heavens cry. Our help is now
Again with your good arm. Will you go
1380 Unperturbed to that unknown place, that place of fear,
To that sin-drenched silence? Seek her out if you dare—
A warrior's reward is warranted by battle,
And treasure, twined gold, torques with jewels,
Your wisdom rewarded if you win your way back."

Twenty-Second Fitt † *Pursuit of Grendel's mother*

Bold Beowulf replied, that brave son of Ecgtheow,
"Sovereign king, do not sorrow—it seems better to me
To finish the feud as friends wreaking vengeance
Than sorrow in silence. We simply decide
To abide and endure and exert valor always,
1390 To find dignity in death. When his days are all done,
The worthiest warrior is well-remembered.
Arise, royal king, let us realize glory,
And tail the tracks of this terrible mother.
I give my good word, she will not get away,

Not in the high hills, or hidden in forests,
Or on the floor of the flood, her flight is all vanity.
But aged king, endure! Await this great outcome,
With patience, empowered, to push through these troubles."
That good and gray king thanked God for His help,
Help merciful and mighty, through that man's great promise.   1400
So Hrothgar's great horse was handled and saddled,
A courser with curled mane. The king rode ahead,
Resplendent and royal, his regulars came after,
Shields on their shoulders. She left clear footprints,
Wide through the woods, with sign easy to track,
A path clear and plain, where she pressed and went through
The marshes and moors, Murder under her arm,
She bore the best thane, the brave Aeschere,
He who with Hrothgar the homeland had ruled.
Then the proud prince passed by the crags,   1410
Down steep defiles, and deep under cliffs,
Narrow, unknown, the noble king led them,
Past crags with caves, crags with trolls.
At the front he fared, a few men with him,
Searching for signs, seeking the trail,
When he saw suddenly on the slope above,
The tendrils of trees tangled on the cliff face,
And a wood filled with woe. The water below
Was bloody and black. The brave Danish cohort,
Faithful friends, and fearless Shieldings all,   1420
Bore bitter heartbreak, the brunt of it there,
For Aeschere's honored head was abandoned here,
Was found on the fell, that fatal place.
That lake surf was surging, the Shieldings saw it,
Heavy with hot blood. A horn, lonely, sounded
A brave battle-cry. That band paused . . .

They watched the water; they saw worms and serpents,
Sea-monsters strange that sounded the depths,
And cold and cruel kraken on the crags basking.
1430 Morning light moved them, the monsters departed,
Went on watery roads, wandering off,
Whether distant or deep, their dangerous way.
Hearing the horn, those hateful beasts dove.
The great prince of the Geats grasped his bow,
And shot with sure aim, the shaft flying true,
Its mark a great monster, striking its middle,
The sharp battle bolt bloodied the water,
As the serpent swam slowly, singled out by death.
The barbed boar-spears with blows repeated
1440 Hooked and held him. Hard death seized him,
Diving down, still dragged to the shore,
A wondrous wave-wanderer. The warriors gazed
At the beast before them. Beowulf prepared
His war gear and weapons, withstanding temptation,
Lest he fear to lose his life to that creature.
His wide mail shirt, woven, in the waters protecting,
Could best guard his body, his bones safeguarding,
Lest the clutch of that cruel one should crack him open,
And have his heart, held with talons.
1450 The helmet for his head was high protection,
And was soon to sink to that swamp bottom,
Entwined with ten jewels, as in times long past,
A smith had slaved on it, and served it up glorious,
A wondrous work by a weapons master.
It was bold in its boar forms, so that no battle frenzy,
Could bite that bright helm, believe it or not.
Unferth was another who offered him help,
Hrothgar's servant and spokesman a sword offered up,

A hilted sword Hrunting, the heft was glorious,
Of ancient heirlooms, easily the best.
Iron at the edge, with eager, dread patterns,
Blood from battle tempered it, brave for a fight.
No hero who held it ever had to retreat,
When attacking, advancing, invading the homeland
To face the foes and fight fierce warriors.
Don't think this daring task was destined as its first.
Unferth, son of Ecglaf, was not eager to fight,
Though stout and strong, and that speech he had uttered,
When doused in drink, had departed from him,
That single swordsman, less strong than the other.
Under the watery waves he would not bet his life
As a loyal lieutenant, so he lost fame and glory,
A boast not lost by Beowulf, the bravest of men,
Who gathered his gear for the grave encounter.

TWENTY-THIRD FITT † *Beowulf fights Grendel's mother*

Brave Beowulf spoke, battle-son of Ecgtheow,
"High heir of Halfdane, hold this in memory,
Great gold-giver, now that I go down to fight,
What was said is settled, sovereign and king—
If killed in this cause, if that comes to pass,
If I lose my life, be loyal still!
Do not fail as a father, be a father to me.
Guard these good men, this gathering of thanes,
These battle-brave men, if this beast should take me.
And the gifts you gave me . . . give them a safe return,
May Hrothgar give to Hygelac that handsome treasure.
The Geat king will gather by the gold without measure,
The son of Hrethel will stare and see those riches,

And gather a good ring-giver gave famous treasures,
And I rejoiced in the jewels and the gems while I could.
1490 Let Unferth enjoy the iron edge I leave to him,
Wave-edged, woven by smithies, woven while molten—
With Hrunting I hunt, in hellish descent
To a deserving destiny, or death will get me."
With these words the Weather-Geat prince,
Impatient with peace, plunged boldly in the mere.
The waiting water enclosed him, welcoming his dive.
It took most of the morning before making the bottom,
Before he felt the floor of that lake.
Soon he sought out that savage mother,
1500 And she sensed right away some man raided her lair.
She had for one hundred winters held this domain,
And sensed the assault, and sought to grasp him.
So she clutched and clawed, when close he approached,
Seized the strong warrior to strike him with talons,
But his mail-shirt held his heart secure,
As the she-devil strained to slaughter-pierce
The links in leather with loathsome claw.
Then this watery wolf, when she touched bottom,
Dragged to her den this doughty lord of those rings,
1510 While he sought and strove his sword to draw,
To wield that weapon against weird sea creatures
That beset him savagely—sea-beasts assailed him,
With sharp tusks they tried to test his mail,
They swarmed him, swimming. Then he saw
He was in some hellish hall, holding off the water.
Where water couldn't reach, no waves could drown him,
A vaulted roof reached up, restraining the flood,
That furious froth. Firelight guttered,
A flickering flame, a faint but clear blaze.

Then he saw that she-devil, that savage wolf-in-the-water,
That monstrous mere-hag. With a main stroke
He spun his strong blade, and struck her foul head.
The blade sang as he swung, a savage war-song.
But the battle-torch would not bite, the brave warrior found
The sword failed to strike, the stroke failed to pierce
Or harm that black heart; the hard blade failed
This man in much need, yet marvels had wrought
In war hand-to-hand, helmets cleaving,
Delivering death to doomed men.
This was the first failure befalling that glory-blade.
But brave Beowulf stood, not buckling in fear,
That high-hearted one, Hygelac's kinsman,
Rejected that wretched sword, though richly embellished—
That thane threw it down, thought to leave it there,
Though strong, made of steel. His own strength he trusted,
His hand-grip of hard might. So high-hearted men should do
When they want to win the warfare brought to them,
Not tangled by troubles, or tension or fears.
He grabbed the great shoulder of Grendel's foul mother,
The great Geat war-lord grasped combat fully.
Filled with great fury, he flung down that monster,
And that deadly demon was brought down to the ground.
She twisted and turned and took him down too,
With her ghastly grasping, she grappled with Beowulf.
Spent with the struggle, he staggered and fell,
Though fierce among fighters, he fell nonetheless.
She chose his great chest as a death chair; she sat,
Drew her great dagger, and down it plunged,
To avenge his last victory, the victim, her son.
The braids linked on his breast bested death that day,
Turning the bitter blade, barring death's entrance.

The heir of Ecgtheow would have accepted death,
Under the wide world, that warrior of Geatland,
Had not that hauberk well-hardened helped turn the blow
But the blessed God of battles brought him deliverance,
The high king of Heaven, the holiest Maker,
The God of goodness gave him this gift;
The great warrior got up, regaining his stance.

TWENTY-FOURTH FITT † *Beowulf kills Grendel's mother in her lair*

He saw a great sword, a slasher from old time,
1560   Ancient doom from the ettins,[7] with an edge well-tempered,
A warrior's war-treasure, a weapon unmatched,
Too hard and heavy to be held by three men
To brandish in battle, in the brunt of war.
It had been forged by fell giants, fashioned to cut.
Our Shielding held that hilt, and hit and struck with it,
Emboldened with battle-lust, that blow was great;
He was wrathful and reckless, his rage was just.
It pierced her proud neck, the point went deep,
Her spine snapped; the blade sliced clean through
1570   Her blotched body, blood went to the floor with her.
His blade was blood-wet, his boast erupted.
Then light lifted the darkness and luminous was the cave,
As when from high heaven there is heat and light
From God's good candle. The great hall he looked over.
He went by the wall, his weapon held high,
Hygelac's thane held it, hoisted in victory,
Still angry, still furious. That sharp edge was useful
To that wise warrior now. He wanted quick restitution
From Grendel, that grim one, for his ghoulish raids,

---

7. Giants.

On the West-Danes in war, in his wicked hate,
More frequently feuding, far more than just once,
When from Hrothgar's hearth-mates he held, and he gripped,
In their sleep he slew them, in slumber they all died.
Fifteen others he fisted, and furiously bore them off,
Doomed men of the Danes, to death he carried them,
A hateful, horrible catch. Our high prince paid him back,
For stone-cold, stretched out, the silent Grendel lay,
Dealt justice by death, and done with his feuds,
Tested in battle, taken from life, with a torn-off arm
In that brave battle at Heorot. That body suffered much,

When desolate in death it endured the last strike.
Beowulf bent over, and his blow severed the head.
Above, wise men waited, watching the surface,
Holding watch with Hrothgar, hating the delay.
The tumbling water tossed, turbid and cloudy,
Blood floated on that bog. The brave counselors knew,
Nodding their gray and good heads, that a great man was gone.
The warrior would not return; they waited in vain.
No return in triumph, no tale of victory
Would be brought from that battle to their king—

The she-wolf of the sea successfully sought out his life.
A nagging wait, the ninth hour came. So noble Shieldings,
Bereaved, left the bluffs; back homeward they went.
The gold-friend of good men left. But the Geats remained,
Staring at the surging blood, sick in their grief,
Their futile wish, their fruitless thought . . . their friend to see again.
Below, that blade began to melt,
In the blood of the battle, a bitter thaw,
A weapon of war went like ice in the springtime;
All of it like ice, every bit of it melted—

Like water ropes unwound when the Father unties them,
Looses the fetters of frost, and frees up the water,

Ruling times and tempests—the true God forever!
The Weder warrior would take nothing away,
Though plenty of precious things were piled around.
He gripped Grendel's head and the great hilt of the sword,
Bedizened and dazzling. The dark blood melted the sword,
Burned up the blade with her blood hot with malice,
The poisonous and polluted blood of the perished she-beast.

1620 Soon that great swimmer, who struggled to victory,
Who bested demons in battle, breasted and kicked his way up.
The currents were cleared, the sea creature was gone,
From that watery waste, since the wandering ghoul
Left this life, lost to this world.
He then swam to the shore, that sailor-protector,
Solid in soul, in the spoil rejoicing,
Holding that head, and the hilt of the sword.
The Geats greeted him gladly as God they all thanked,
That band of brave warriors, who believed him now,

1630 Seeing him sound and safe in return.
Soon that hero's helmet and heavy mail shirt
Were taken as the tale was told. The bog returned,
Subsiding to silence, the stain of blood still there.
Lighthearted they left, looking to the paths back,
High in their hearts, their heads held high,
As they reckoned the road. Real men
Carried that craggy head from the cliff at the shore,
A strain for strong men, a solid haul,
A feat for the faithful, since four men carried it

1640 Placed on pole, impaled on a spear,
To get Grendel's great head to the gold-hall of Heorot.
So marching in their might, these men of valor came
To the hall-doors of Heorot, high-hearted Geats,
In formation as for fighting. Their feudal lord

Marched with these men, across meadows in pride.
Then that warrior walked in, welcome to the hall,
Fearless and famed, a fighter in truth,
A hard man, head high, and Hrothgar was greeted.
Grendel's head was hauled, by the hair it was hauled
Into the hall where heroes sit. Grendel's head was dragged,   1650
A marvelous sight to men of birth, a marvel to the queen,
A shocking sight; they stared in awe.

TWENTY-FIFTH FITT † *Beowulf recounts story, hilt*

Beowulf broke out, that brave son of Ecgtheow,
"See this sundered head, son of Halfdane,
Lord and leader of Shieldings, we love what we've brought,
These tokens of triumph; take it all in.
I strove in my spirit, saving my life
Through warfare in water, a great work was done
In struggle and strain, my strength was waning,
My fight was failing, faltering . . . had the Lord not saved me.   1660
I held in both hands Hrunting the sword
And that weapon of war is worthy and good,
But the Ruler of all realms gave a reckoning kindness
When I saw a sword hanging in splendor and brightness,
Gigantic and good—God guided me to it,
A friend to the friendless—so I fought with it,
Felling those fearsome ones, fate was behind me,
Slaying with that sword the sentries both there.
The blade burned up when the blood touched it,
In the heat of hot battle; the hilt is here with me   1670
From my enemies, adversaries. I avenged their wickedness,
The death of good Danes, due as straight justice.
I can tell you truly that we've taken Heorot back,

Now safe to sleep in with your soldiers and thanes,
All your people, all your folk, everyone from the tribe,
Whether young or old; no aching fear,
Lord and leader of Shieldings, will leap from darkness again,
Dealing dark death that you dared not confront."
Then the great gold hilt was given to the gray-beard,
1680 Placed in the hand of the hero, who held it in joy.
Giant smiths sought to forge it, they summoned their craft.
After the downfall of demons, the Danish lord took it,
The work of wise smith-craft, the world being free
Of that grotesque ghoul, God's mortal foe,
Murdering monster, and his mother with him.
It passed into possession of the people's great lord,
The best king between all boundaries of the seas,
Who gave out his gold, good gifts throughout Scandia.
Hrothgar held forth—with the hilt in his hand,
1690 That ancient heirloom of old, with etchings and runes
From the day of great doom when a devastating flood,
A wall of great waves wiped out the giants.
Their fight was futile, their fate was determined,
Strangers to God, sunk in their sin, scores were settled by God,
When with a rush the Ruler wrecked them with water.
On the hilt of that heavy gold, on the handgrip from old times,
Were runes wisely written, and the runes described
For whom the snake-bladed sword was singly wrought,
The best of all blades from bygone days,
1700 That Titans' hilt well entwined. The tall king spoke,
The high-hearted son of Halfdane. The hall was silent:
"Now I tell the truth, the tale may be told,
A man mindful of truth may say in all honesty,
That this man is mighty, and his marvelous strength
Belongs to the best, who battles have won.

Your fame, my great friend, will go farther than all.
Beowulf the brave will be the boast of all nations.
You will keep your signal strength with simplicity of wisdom.
My love, a king's constant, will keep you, sustain you.
In coming years, danger creeping, you will keep your people,   1710
A hero to help them. Heremod was not that way,
The heir of Ecgwela, the Honor-Shieldings' lord,
Who did not grow great for their good, but for gruesome killing,
Death for Danes, doom from their own king.
Heart-swollen, hateful, his own hall filled with blood,
Killing table-companions! So that king passed alone,
Exiled for his anger, excluded from gladness.
Though that man was mighty, by his Maker endowed,
Given power and purpose, yet pride crept in.
Though favored and fortunate, he was fierce in his greed.   1720
His heart-hoard expanded, and he hardly gave rings
To the Danes as their due; he died as he lived, joyless,
After suffering and straining, after struggling for nothing,
To hurt his own hall. Here is the lesson—
Let virtue lead you. This life teaches much,
For those wise from many winters. The wonder is great—
How God Almighty is good, giving grace to men,
How His Spirit gives strength in the sending of wisdom,
Wealth, or wide holdings. He wields all things.
The Ruler of all realms gives riches to some,   1730
Lets a high-hearted hero hold onto adventures,
Gives him holdings and halls, and high thrones in them.
Strongholds, sure fortresses are secure in his hand,
Treasures, great tracts of land, and towers are his,
A valiant kingdom so vast, with vanity is invisible,
And a lackwit with no wisdom cannot weather a crisis.
So he rules from feast to feast, with fate slowly stalking him,

No sickness, no sadness, no shadows to trouble him,
No malevolent malice mars his banquets,
1740 No swords are sharpened, no soldiers muster against him.
The world hears his will, and willingly follows him,

Twenty-Sixth Fitt † *Hrothgar admonishes and retires*

"Until concealed pride is conceived and contrives to grow,
Wakens and widens, while the watchman sleeps on,
That sentry of the soul. His sleep is too deep,
And masters his mind; the murderer creeps closely,
In evil his arrows are aimed with his bow.
He is hit, although helmeted, his heart is pierced,
A shaft shatters him; no shelter available
From the wicked little whispers of this worm-tongued fiend.
1750 What he long held as luxury seems little to him now,
Greedy for gold, he gives no more rings,
Savage and sullen, the summoning fate
He doubts and despises, and the debt God gave him,
That Worker of wonders, giving wealth, fame, and glory.
But the end arrived, the entrance of doom,
When the frail frame of the body in fragility surrendered,
Fated to fall, and fearless raiders come
To pillage and plunder the proud king's old jewels,
The riches of royalty, the ruins of pride.
1760 So Beowulf, friend, ban such thoughts. Better be humble,
As the best of brave men, the better part take—
Eternal gains, everlasting life; arrogance is death,
Famed warrior and friend. The flower of your youth
Was strength sustained, but soon it will be
That sickness or sword-stroke will slice it clean from you,
Or the flickering flames, or a flood swelling banks,

Or a blade's bitter slash, or the brunt of a spear,
Or loathsome old age, or your eyes start to go,
Dimming in darkness. Death is surefooted
And will run to this reckoning, though the runes are heroic.
Without faltering, for fifty long years I furnished the Danes
With wealth through great warfare, and warded off foes,
Many and mighty from middle-earth over,
By sword and spear, by strength and main,
No foe was formidable enough to fight under the sun.
But fate twisted and turned on me, night terror beset us,
Grief came to grind us when Grendel arose
To harrow this hall, a hellish enemy.
Those raids nigh ruined us, unresting, tormented,
Heavy and heart-sick. But Heaven is good,   1780
The eternal and everlasting God extended our lives,
That I after this evil have eyes that can rest
On this hilt and that head, cut hard from his shoulders!
Join your comrades in joy, jubilant, triumphant,
A warrior of worth! Wealth will come in a torrent
When day dawns, and your due shall be yours."
The Geat prince was glad and gained his honors,
He sought out his seat as the sage king required.
Then again, as before gathered, these good men all feasted,
Their courage contained, coiled and ready,   1790
High-hearted in the hall. The helmet of night came,
Dusk then deepened. Those daring ones rose,
So the grizzled and gray-headed would go to their rest,
The strong Shielding and the splendid Geat,
Though sturdy and strong for sleeping longed.
He was a furious fighter, a famed wanderer
From far away, so a favored courtier led them,
Who with pride and polish provided courtly care,

Such as told well with travelers when they tired of the road,
1800 Or of the swan-road, the sea, when spent with their journey.
That great guest slept under gables of gold,
And his sleep was sound; safety reigned in the hall.
Until bright calls from the blackbird gave the best of the morning,
With a splendid sunrise. Light spread everywhere,
Shining followed shadows. The shield-Geats hurried;
Those earls were eager to exit homeward,
To get back to blessed hearth, and their bold warrior leader
Wished to steer his ship toward their summoning homes.
Beowulf had brought back the blade called Hrunting
1810 To Unferth son of Ecglaf, and urged him to take it,
That splendid sword, and swore he was thankful;
He considered it a keen blade, constant in battle.
Its weakness in warfare he would not mention,
How the iron edge failed, an empty try—a high-hearted man.
Impatient for parting, present in armor,
The warriors were waiting, while he went to the king,
That throne dear to the Danes. The daring warrior
Came to the high seat of Hrothgar and hailed him warmly.

Twenty-Seventh Fitt † *Beowulf's farewell, gifts referred to*

Bold Beowulf spoke, brave son of Ecgtheow—
1820 "We seafaring sailors would now say our desire,
To return from this trip and treasure bring to Hygelac.
Here in this hall we found a host well-suited;
Well-treated, taken care of, our tale will praise you.
If by fighting my fealty can fasten more strongly
So that your love, great lord, will lift ever higher,
Than I have done through my deeds in desperate adventures,
Know I am willing for war, still willing to fight.

If I should hear, across the high seas, that hostile neighbors
Have attacked and assaulted to engage you in battle,
As they have persecuted in the past, to place their feet in your hall . . .
Thousands of thanes I thence shall bring,
Great heroes to help you. Hygelac will help,
Guardian prince of his people, he will press to your aid,
Though in truth he is tender, he will tell with his bravery
By both word and battle, that bold I might serve you,
Bringing weapons of war to win you the victory,
Fresh troops to your trial, from our tested alliance.
If Hrethric visits Hygelac, the hall of the Geats,
He can count on our king, and a court full of friends.
A victor should visit adventuresome lands,
Many men will be mindful of a man who is strong."
Hrothgar answered him, holding forth like a king,
"These good words are God's, He gave them to you,
Heaven-sent to your soul! Such sagacious counsel
From a seer so young, so strong in mind and body.
That greatness in a grasp, and good with your mind,
You are wise with words. I wonder not
If Hrethel's heir should die, hurt fatally in battle,
By spear, or sword, or struck some other way,
By illness or empty herbs, and your elder and prince should die,
And he rests, returning to dust, and life remains for you—
There is no better choice as chieftain chosen from the Sea-Geats,
Than you, despite youth, than you for their king.
The Geats—a hoard-guard of heroes, if you held the throne,
Lord over your own land. Your life pleases me
The more I meditate on it, the more I know you, Beowulf!
You have brought a bond for both our peoples,
For sons of Geats, sons of Danes, spearmen both,

Shall now pursue peace, and pull away from strife,
1860 And the wars we once waged, as our warriors learn restraint.
As long as I live, as long as I rule here,
Let us take our turns as treasure is exchanged,
As we greet with gifts across the gannet's-bath and home,
And the ring-prowed riders bear ring-proud givers,
With tokens of our trust. I take it in faith
That our friends and foes will be faced together
As we hold in honor the health of the ancient ways."
So in the hall of Halfdane's heir, Hrothgar offered riches
Twelve great treasures, and told him farewell,
1870 Bidding him to bear them home to his beloved land,
To sail home safely, and soon to return.
Then the kindly king kissed him warmly,
The Shieldings' sovereign in sorrow embraced him,
Took his neck and held tight. The tears flowed
From the great and gray-headed king, the good Hrothgar.
He held to this hope, though heavy with winters,
That God would give him a greeting chance once more,
To hear this Geat in his hall. This hero was dear to him.
His chest was tight, a tempest there brought tears from the deep,
1880 His sorrow of soul had a secret hall,
Bound in breast, for that beloved man
Burned in his blood. Then Beowulf departed,
Glorious in gold, the grass under his feet,
His gestures rejoicing. His good ship waited,
Kept by the cold anchor, its captain awaiting.
They bent their way toward the beach, they blessed Hrothgar's gifts,
They praised him repeatedly. He was a prince without peer,
Beloved and blameless, until broken by years,
His splendid strength taken, as years spare no man.

Twenty-Eighth Fitt † *Beowulf sails, bad queen, Geatland refurbished*

These warriors came wending their way to the coast,　　　　1890
Brave-hearted and bold, bearing their armor,
Links of battle-metal, burnished bright in their triumph,
The coast-guard courageous kept them in view,
From the brow of the bluff no boasting taunts came,
Or reached the riders as the guard rode to meet them.
He welcomed the warriors, those Weders who came,
Bright-armored brave fighters, believing in joy.
The ship on the strand was seaworthy and wide,
Laden with riches, ring-prowed, riding at anchor.
The tall-masted treasure ship, to take the wealth homeward,　　1900
Rose high over the hoard-gold that Hrothgar had given.
Beowulf gave their boat-guard a blade bound in gold,
A present of pride on the plank in the mead-hall,
He was esteemed and honored, that ancient blade with him.
Then their keel carved water, they caught the wind,
And drove the deep water with Denmark behind them.
They hoisted high the wind-coat and held it with ropes,
Tight to the tall mast; their timbers creaked.
The wind behind worked them, that wave-skimmer flew,
Steady and sure, speeding toward home,　　　　　　1910
Foam-throated she flew, fleet like an arrow.
Her bow cut the currents, and kept her on course,
Till coming they caught sight of the cliffs of the Geats,
The headlands of home. Hard the boat drove,
Brought by blustering winds to the beach proudly.
The harbor-guard held watch, holding hope for return,
Waiting long for loved warriors, who had left for Denmark.
By the water he waited and watched a long time.
The ship, broad in the beam, was bound to the shore,

1920 With the right anchor-ropes, resisting the surf,
Lest those long-trusted timbers should tear themselves loose.
Then Beowulf beckoned, "Bear this treasure ashore."
There were gems, and gold, and goodly amounts more,
That were gifts all to go to the giver of rings,
Hygelac, son of Hrethel, in his hall by the sea,
Close to the cliffed sea-wall, a kingly estate.
That hall was high, his haven was splendid,
A majestic king, magnificent, his queen marvelous,
Hygd was wise and well-spoken, though her winters were few
1930 In that formidable fortress where she found herself.
Haereth's high-hearted daughter, she held to high standards,
And gave out great gifts to the Geats of their court.
Thryth's pride was not present in her, Hygd prevailed with kindness,
Unlike that cruel queen who with crimes held sway.
Though dauntless, none dared look on her, however deep his courage.
Only her lord, he alone, of all the men at court
Could look on that lady her likeness to see.
Fetters would fasten him and find his doomed madness,
A black and dark bondage. A brief wait passed
1940 And a burnished blade brought an end to his life,
The penalty pronounced to the people assembled.
The custom of queens should not come to this—
A peace-weaver punishing? Pursuing blood?
Demanding more wrath, murdering warriors?
A man's life lost, left desolate for nothing?
But Hemming's high kinsman held back her ways.
Ale drinkers agreed and also told tales;
Her outrages, her onslaughts, her eager cruelties
Were made less, diminished, when she made her journey,
1950 Going as bride gold-bedecked to a good hero and prince,
A high and haughty noble in the hall of Offa.

Over the foaming flood at her father's wish,
She sought her new home safely, and since then flourished
In great royal riches and a regal throne,
Fitted by fate for the fame she was given,
She loved long and hard that lord of warriors.
Of all the high heroes he was honored the most,
From sea to sea, excelling all others.
Presented with praise for his power in war,
Offa fought fiercely freeing his homeland.   1960
That warrior worked as a king, wisely he reigned
Over the extent of his kingdom. Eomer his son
Was a help of heroes and Hemming's kinsman,
Grandson of Garmund and great in warfare.

Twenty-Ninth Fitt † *Hygelac receives Beowulf, Freawaru warning*

Beowulf crossed the beach, his best warriors with him,
The wide sea-strand was silently waiting for them.
The world-candle warmed them, wending its southern course;
Their steps were strong. They strode along
To the place their prince waited, to their protector they went,
Where the brave young battle-king in his beautiful hall,   1970
King truly, keeper and giver of rings, killer of Ongentheow,
In his fortress for fighters. To famous Hygelac
Beowulf's return was told, the tale ran ahead—
There in the king's court where kinsmen take refuge,
His shield-friend was safe, both sound and alive,
And he walked, well and joyful, welcomed through the yards.
The high king of the hall ordered hasty preparations,
And space for these strong ones was soon made ready.
He sat by his sovereign, returned safe from adventure,
Kinsman with kin. His kingly lord   1980

Had greeted him graciously, and given him welcome
With earnest, ordered formal words. The ale was flowing
When Haereth's high-hearted daughter through the hall entered.
She was a friend to fighters, and filled up their cups,
Held up by those heroes. Hygelac then asked
His comrade questions and kept on asking—
In the high-beamed hall—hungry to know
Their adventures, their odyssey, how eager for battle they were.
"What came of your call, my kinsman Beowulf,
1990 When you jumped to the journey to join with the Danes
Over the salty sea, seeking to do battle,
Hellish warfare in Heorot? Could you help their king,
Lift the grief of their great chief, give aid to Hrothgar
In his well-known woe? Waves of sorrow
Surged in my sadness; I saw disaster coming
To my good friend's greatness, I gave many requests
That you not go to grapple with Grendel's bloody claws,
But to cede to the South-Danes the settlement of that fight,
Let them give battle to Grendel! But God be thanked
2000 For your safe return, sound, and sitting beside me."
Then brave Beowulf spoke, the best son of Ecgtheow—
"O Hygelac, what happened is hardly obscure,
Many men have heard it, that mashed meeting we had,
That great and grim battle between Grendel and me,
Which we held in the hall where his hatred would vent
When he slaughtered Shielding-Victors, sending them grief,
Misery after misery. I made all that right.
No spawn of that sin-creature can spin out a boast,
None that now live, for that night war before dawn,
2010 Can boast of that battle, for beaten were they,
As I fought that vile flesh. But first was an audience,

I went to Hrothgar's great hall, to hale that ring-giver,
Halfdane's high kinsman, on his hall-throne victorious.
As soon as he saw that I sought out this purpose,
He soon seated me with his son and his heir.
As I love this good life—his lieutenants were valiant,
Such mead made from honey, and merry laughter,
I have not heard under heaven! His high-hearted queen,
Wealhtheow, peace-weaver, wove through the hall,
Encouraged the kinsmen, and gave clasps and rings.   2020
She then sought out her seat and summoned more gifts.
Hrothgar's daughter, dark beauty, would dance through the rows,
Offering ale to earls in their turn.
Her name was known to us, not obscure to hall-warriors.
Freawaru was that fitting name, as the fine gold cup
She extended and offered. Engaged she was,
That gold-decked damsel, to the dauntless son of Froda.
The Shielding-king sought this, as it seemed wise to him,
To keep safe his kingdom; he considered it prudent
To make fast a marriage and master the feuds,   2030
Stop the slaughtering. But seldom it happens,
When someone was slain, that the spears may rest,
Though the bride be beautiful, but a brief time.
The Heathobards may hate it, at the hall wedding feast,
When Ingeld enters, his arm offered to that woman.
And the Danes, dauntless all, dared to bring heirlooms,
Escorting the eager peace-weaver from the entrance to their seats,
And on their hips are those heirlooms, old Heathobard treasures,
Hilted and hard, high treasures, ring-decked,
Weapons of war that they wielded at one time   2040
Until they lost their linden-shields, and lives not a few,
On the fields of fighting, with their final losses.

"Then some old captain in his cups will catch a glimpse
Of an ancient heirloom, and, being old, he remembers
The spear-death of his soldiers—he smolders in anger—
His cold heart turns cruel, he catches a young eye,
And tries his temper, tests his resolve.
He awakens old wars with whispering words:
'Comrade, can you not see? Did you catch that sword's glint?
2050 That was the weapon which your father carried
To his final fight, in that feud from old times,
That bravest of blades, when the battle-Danes took him,
When Wethergeld fell in war and the waste of that loss
Was our heroes' hurt at the hands of the Shieldings?
So here is the *son* of that swaggering Dane,
Proud in his pacing, presumptuous in conceit,
He rejoices in your jealousy, and that jeweled hilt carries
On his hateful hip, that blade should be held, rightfully, by you.'
So he aggravates and urges and eggs on that warrior
2060 With sharp and shrewd words till the shameful moment
When Freawaru's fallen thane, for his father's war deed,
Is battered in blood and a blade splits him open,
His life entirely lost. The lieutenant assassin flees;
He knows that cold country and can find secret paths.
Peace is broken on both sides, and battle looms,
Their oaths are not owned when Ingeld's breast heats up,
Filling with fury, wanting to fight, not love,
And his care for his peace-queen grow cooler and wanes.
So why hold up high the Heathobards' faith,
2070 Their debt to the Danes, or their enduring trust
And purchase of peace? But let us pass on from this,
Turning again to Grendel, that you may grasp the story,

O royal ring-giver, and the results of that fight,
That hand-battle with hell. When heaven's jewel
Had crossed the clear sky, that cruel monster came,
That dread bringer of death, to deal out his malice
Where still sound enough we set our watch for the hall.
That hater seized Hondscio, with his hands tore him up,
He was fated to fall. He was first to die;
Grendel gobbled him, that belt-girded warrior,   2080
Our good and gracious thane was gripped in death,
And that brave man's body was bolted down.
Yet Grendel wouldn't go from that golden hall,
Eagerly chewing entrails but still empty-handed.
His mind full of murder, and his maw with bloody teeth,
So he grabbed me greedily and got as good as he gave,
Though his presence was powerful. A pouch hung by his side,
Cunningly made with clasps, and kept tight with bands,
A wondrous work devised, in black wisdom wrought,
By dark and devilish arts from dragon pelts.   2090
He thought to throw me in, though an innocent man,
That fatal loathsome fiend would fight to thrust me in
With many other men. He might have prevailed
Had I not suddenly stood to strike him back in anger.
My tale would take too long if I told the whole story,
How I paid that predator back, a grave penalty for his deeds.
But I proved in that place, dear prince, your people's honor,
My fighting gained fame. His flight clattered out
To a little more life, the less the better.
But the wreck of his right arm remained in the hall,   2100
Held by us in Heorot. That hellish one fled
To die in the darkness on the deep ocean floor.
The Shielding friend said that the struggle was worth
The gifts he would give, gold in plenty,

Treasure untold, when the tall dawn came,
And we gratefully gathered in the great mead-hall.
There were stories, then songs, and a Shielding, gray-headed,
Battle tested, battle tried, told of the old times.
Then suddenly some hero would sing with his harp,
2110 His chanting-word chosen to sing cheerful lays,
With sad songs as well, all settled in truth,
Amazing and marvelous. The majestic king
Told tales from his youth, told of times long past,
When he could strike with strength, but now struggled with age,
A gray-headed great one; his good heart ached,
As his mind mulled over those melted battle marvels.
So in the hall of Heorot, the whole of that day,
We talked and we tasted until the night fell.
Grendel's mother mauled us, another murder to deal with.
2120 She sought victory in vengeance, vile in malice;
Her son was slain, she sought his killers,
Got revenge on the Geats. Grendel's mother monstrous
Fell in a fury and fought with us there,
Avenged her son on Aeschere, attacked that good counselor,
That loyal thane lost his life, his light was gone.
When the morning mist came, our mourning was broken,
When the Danes could not deal with this death by their custom—
His body could not be burned, that best warrior advisor.
Away under the water, wailing and cackling,
2130 She carried that corpse in the clutch of a fiend.
Hrothgar, heavy-hearted, was hurt beyond speaking.
That burden almost broke him, that brave lord of his people.
That great prince implored me, pleaded with anguish,
To seek the sea's bottom and summon up vengeance,
To brave that beast's power, take battle down to her,
For goodness and glory and great honor with men.

He would richly reward me. I resolved to fight, it is known,
And found that fierce monster on the floor of the sea.
The hand-battle was hard, her foul hall was the place
Where blood soaked the brine and bespattered the walls. 2140
With a high-hilted blade I took her head off,
From Grendel's grotesque mother, and gained my own life,
I barely bested her—my brave end was not yet.
Then Halfdane's son, Hrothgar, that helper of warriors,
Gave great gifts to me, both gear and fine riches.

THIRTY-FIRST FITT † *Beowulf loyal to Hygelac, becomes king of Geats*

"So this king kept faith, the customs of old,
And I lacked for little. No lesser gifts were offered
The recompense and reward were righteous—true gifts
From Halfdane's heir, which I have from him.
Now to you, my prince and pride, I present them all, 2150
I give them all gladly. Your goodness alone
Is my favor and fealty. Few others I have
As kinsmen this close, except, kind Hygelac, you."
The boar-head standard brought, Beowulf presented it,
And a high helmet for war, and a hauberk gray,
A sword of splendor, then speaking he said,
"This weaponry and war-gear was wisely given
By Hrothgar, that hero, and holding it out,
He said that its story should straightway be told you—
King Heorogar held it, heroic in battle, 2160
Lord for a long time, in the land of the Shieldings,
Did not bequeath this corselet with the crown to his son,
That is, Heoroweard, dauntless and daring, as dear as he was.
This best battle-harness—may blessings attend it!"
I then heard that four horses in harness and valiant,

Dappled and daring, decked out in trappings,
Each one like the others, eager for battle,
He gave his good prince. So great-hearted kinsmen
Should not weave with wiles, or work in craftiness,
2170　Or with deep deceptiveness bring death out of hiding.
This nephew and neighbor was never treacherous
To Hygelac the high-hearted, holding him dear.
Both of them believed in what was best for the other.
I heard, too, of the torque, a treasure for Hygd,
A wonderful gift, wrought gold, which Wealhtheow gave to him,
A mild daughter of majesty—three mettlesome steeds also,
High-stepping horses, with hand-wrought leather saddles.
Bright on her breast was that bright torque of the queen's.
The son of Ecgtheow showed his settled heart,
2180　As a man known for nobility, and not for malice.
High honor was his; in the hall of ale he would not
Kill his comrades, free from cruelty in heart,
Although among men, his might was the greatest,
A gift from God, that glorious strength,
Above all brave warriors. Belittled a long time
As worthless by warriors, as weak by the Geats.
His prince wouldn't pick him, his power unseen,
His favor failed him in the feasting hall.
Slothful and slack the stronger men thought him,
2190　A prince far too passive, no promise at all.
But real change was chosen when the chance arose.
Then the brave bulwark king bade them bring a treasure,
Hrethel's heirloom, hilt covered with gold,
A blade embellished, no better anywhere,
A treasure in truth, a trust with the Geats.
That bright blade was laid on Beowulf's knees,
And holdings from Hygelac, measured in hides, seven thousand,

With a hall and high seat. These holdings were common,
But the birthright of both was best for the king,
Because his rule in the realm was right and unquestioned,   2200
Until the Geat king gave it as a good gift of honor.
Now it was left to him later by the levying years,
Proud Hygelac perished through the penalty of war,
And Heardred with Hygelac, by the hard blades of battle,
Under the sheltering shield-wall that slaughter left them,
When the fighting Swedish foe found them defending
The good Geat townships with great courage.
They hunted Hereric's nephew and hurt him in battle.
So Beowulf the brave a broad realm came to rule
As defender for fifty winters, and was found to rule well,   2210
As head and high prince he held the throne,
A wise and wizened king until the worm came,
A deadly raging dragon from the depths of night.
In the heathery hills a hidden treasure lay,
In a stone cave on a craggy slope. A straight path ran there,
A hidden mountain hold. But a hurrying man
Came to that cave and crept inside
To that heathenish hoard. His hand soon found
A cup encrusted with gems, which he kept as he left.
The thief slipped away silently from the sleeping worm,   2220
But soon great sorrow descended on the villages—
They felt the wrath and the rage of the rampaging dragon.

THIRTY-SECOND FITT † *Dragon is disturbed and advances*

That churl did not choose a chance at the treasure,
He did not want to lay waste to the ways of his people,
But in peril, pursued, some prince's slave,
Had fled from a flogging, in fear sought out shelter,

Crept into that cave, quite conscious of sinning.
When he entered, not eagerly, the awful spectacle
Shook him, seized him, and sent him reeling,
2230 Yet that fool and fugitive felt in hand something
And in his frightful flight his feet took him out,
With the treasure cup taken, and our last tale with it.
There were many other marvels, magnificent treasure,
Honored heirlooms in this earth hall were stored
By some ancient adventurer, an earl with great treasure,
Leaving this legacy as the last of his race,
Cunningly hidden, craftily stored, a cave to receive it,
Dark below, deep in the ground. Death had taken the others,
And he alone, last hero, had hidden the gold,
2240 He alone was left alive from that tribe,
Mourning his men, missing them deeply,
While the reward his delight, that wonderful treasure,
Was his bitter-love—*briefly*. That burial spot, ready,
Near the shore of the sea, secure on the headland,
Its location was left secret, lost to all others,
And he laid lordly treasures, leaving them there,
The heavy gold heaped and hidden from view
By that guardian of gold rings. He gave up few words:
"Now keep it, earth cave, keep it far from all heroes,
2250 This treasure untold, and their tales buried with it.
Good men grasped it before, but war got them finally,
Cruelly taking my kin, to keep them in death,
To rob them of riches, and the richness of life.
No liegemen are left, who loved honor and battle,
No hall-joy, high singing, no holding our cups,
Bright with mead-blessing. My brave men are lost.
Their hardened helmets which held golden sections,
Shall have plates fall apart. The polishing servants

Who burnished their brightness, for battle preparing,
Have died, and in death are done with their labors. 2260
The same with their shields, the same with their mail,
No resisting the rust that rots out this armor.
No more mail off to battle with that marauding chieftain,
On the back of that brave one. No blessed harp music,
No songs from the strong wood. No spiraling hunter,
No hawk through the hall, no horses champing and stamping
In the king's ancient courtyard. The cruelty of death
Swept these sons of men down that sorrowful river."
With a mind full of mourning, he murmured his grief,
Alone, the last one, he took leave of them all, 2270
He wept day to dusk, until death's surging tide
Swept over his sorrow. That serpent and worm
Found the hoard that was hidden, that heathen gold,
Who, with burning breath, found the barrow at midnight,
Firedrake, flame-snake, a foul dragon with wings,
Enveloped in vice and fire, the villages below
Fear that fantastic worm. It is his fate to seek out treasure,
Hidden hoards, all that heathenish gold,
Which he guards in his guile, and gets nothing from it.
For three hundred thorough winters, that worm stayed hidden, 2280
Holding his hoard in that hall down below,
Poisonous, powerful, till a purloining slave
Kindled his cruelty, and took a cup to his master,
As a price for his peace, approaching his lord,
With the booty for bond. That barrow was pilfered,
Pardon was promised . . . with the penalty coming,
A wretched return—but his ruler still saw
A catch of great cunning, a cup from the old days.
When the drake was done sleeping, dark woes were kindled.
He sniffed along stones and slithered outside, 2290

Finding a footprint of the fellow just gone,
Who had stupidly stepped by the serpent's great head.
So may the lucky in life leave disaster behind,
Whether exile or agony, when the Almighty pleases
To defend them with favor, though feckless they be.
That guardian of gold over ground went sniffing
For the miserable man who made off with that cup.
Aflame with fierce anger he flew from his barrow,
Cruelty over the crags, a comfortless land,
2300 No one walked in that wilderness, yet for warfare he lusted,
And the blood of battle. The barrow he searched again,
That fine cup to find, and finally discovered
That some miserable mortal had manhandled his treasure,
His gems and his gold that he guarded in malice.
Impatient, petulant, till past the sundown,
Boiling with black rage was that barrow drake—
They would pay the penalty, punished with flame
For dear drinking cup's loss. Now day was gone
As the drake had desired; he dove from his wall,
2310 No longer lingering, but lusting with fire,
Enfolded by flames, a fright from the skies,
For the residents of that realm, their ruin soon coming,
And the grief of their good lord, and his grievous death.

THIRTY-THIRD FITT † *Dragon attacks, Beowulf believes he offended God*

Then that beast, belching fire, burst down upon them,
Burning bright homes. The blazes stood out,
Struck fear in falling spirits. That fatal monster
Left no living thing, leaving burnt-out homes.
His fired ferocity and fighting malice
Was widely witnessed, how that winged serpent

Hounded and harried the hearts of the Geats.
A grim giver of grief to those good people.
At dawn, his hidden hoard was a haven for him.
His flames of fire had enfolded the people
In a blaze of burning. To his barrow he retreated,
His bulwark for battle—a belief that was empty.
Beowulf was brought the blunt truth straightway,
Death and danger arrived. His dear homeland threatened,
The best of his buildings in the burning had melted,
With the great throne of the Geats. That good king
Was sorrowful and sad, sunken in spirit.
That wise king worried that the World-Ruler
Brought down righteous wrath for an old right violated,
Testing and trying the Lord. His tempted breast with
Black thoughts boiled, as before had not been.
That fiery drake's flame had flattened their stronghold;
From the cliffs of the coast, continuously inland,
From the beach to the bluffs, but their battling king,
A wise prince of the Weders, worked out a plan.
A massive metal shield was made by his instruction,
Entirely of iron—that earl in wisdom knew
That a wooden war-shield would be worthless,
So with cunning craft they cast his marvel,
Lest they lose linden to flame. The life of that prince
Was soon to suffer the sorrows of death,
His days diminishing, and the dragon also,
Though his greed and that gold had gone long together.
The ring-giver reckoned it a wretched shame
To fight that far-flyer with a fierce host of men,
A boastful band of men; battle did not frighten him,
The dragon's dread presence he deemed a small thing,
Its vicious foul vigor and its violence threatening.

He had seen such things before, and struggles of war,
Conquest in combat, the cleansing of Heorot,
That great hall of Hrothgar's, which his hand had freed,
When his grip had killed Grendel, and in grappling took out
That fierce and foul clan. That fighter also did well
In the hard war, hand-fighting, when Hygelac fell,
When the Geat ruler of right in the roil of battle,
That high son of Hrethel, heaved his last breath,
2360   Because of hard sword strokes slashing in Frisia,
Beaten down by blades. Beowulf fled that place
Through skill in swimming and the strength of his arms,
Taking thought for thirty mail coats, thinking to escape
With those coats to the coast—so he came to the sea.
No great tale for the tribe of Hetware, no telling vaunt,
As they came to that contest and carried the fight to him,
Their bucklers were battered, and blades lost—
Few of those fighters found their way back home.
Eager for home, Ecgtheow's son entered the sea and swam,
2370   Forlorn and lonely, his land to seek.
There Hygd held an offer of both hoard and realm,
Rings and a royal-throne—reason told her
That her son had no strength to save that great throne
From hostile heathen after Hygelac's fall.
But in a blow to the bereaved tribe, Beowulf would not
Accept the rule or royal sway over his rightful lord's heir,
Young Heardred, son of Hygelac, that high-born prince.
He supported his sovereign and served him in honor,
A true friend with all fealty and favorable counsel,
2380   Until abler, grown older, he accepted full governance
Of the warlike Weder-Geats. The water brought exiles
Seeking his support—they were sons of Ohthere.
They were rebels against the rule of the royal Swede king,

A shield of Scylfings, a sea-king of fame,
A giver of gold, a great, mighty prince.
So Heardred fell hard, hospitable prince,
And he perished in pain from a piercing sword,
From the blow of a blade, that boy-king of Hygelac.
Ongentheow's eager son, Onela, departed
For hearth and home after Heardred was killed,   2390
Leaving Beowulf behind, a brave lord for the Geats,
To give gold, and wise guidance—a *good* king that was!

Thirty-Fourth Fitt † *Beowulf hunts dragon in sorrow and despair*

The death of his dear prince he desired to avenge,
And gave a gift to Eadgils, a group of soldiers,
Reinforcements for a friend, to fortify resolve.
Over the waves, over water, to Ohthere's son,
Both warriors and weapons came. He won his revenge
When the king was killed after care-ridden raids.
So through struggles many the son of Ecgtheow
Had persevered, and passed through perils abundant   2400
With dauntless daring, until *this* day arrived,
That destined the deed of the fire-drake battle.
With eleven others the aged lord of Geats
Stood firm, stirred in his anger, and sought out the dragon.
He had heard the whole story, how the harm had arisen,
The maiming of men. That marvelous cup
Had been brought to Beowulf and bestowed on him.
A thirteenth man, the thief, they had thought to bring along,
The one who stirred the strife and started everything,
A cringing captive, that careworn slave.   2410
Fearful, but forced, he found the path up
To the earth-mound entrance, and the edge of battle,

Where breakers dashed the barrow on the bluff near the sea,
A sea that was surging. Inside was the treasure,
Of glittering gold-work—and a glaring dragon,
Fierce and formidable, filled with gold-yearning,
He lurked in his lust. That lair was forbidding,
No easy entrance for arms to win.
That heroic high king on the headland sat down
2420 And spoke solemn words to succor his men,
As a Geat king, gold-giver. Grim was his heart,
Wavering, but wonderful. Wyrd was upon him,
And was ready to reach that righteous man,
Hunt down his hoard-soul, and halve it in two,
His breath from his body. That bold prince's life
Would no longer linger, and would be lost from his body.
Beowulf spoke boldy, that brave son of Ecgtheow—
"I have sought out struggles; I certainly fought
Through terrible troubles. I have tales from my youth.
2430 My royal Geat ruler gave me riches of friendship,
Summoned me when seven, and sought to raise me.
King Hrethel then had me, a hall-friend from my father,
Gave me food for the feasting and the favor of kinship.
My life there, I was not least—he liked me as well,
No better than his birthright sons, no less blessed than them either—
Herebeald and Haethcyn and Hygelac my lord.
The eldest untimely died from an unwitting arrow,
A kinsman's cruel mistake, caused his bier to come early,
When Haethcyn's cursed hand from the horned bow slipped,
2440 And a feathered arrow flew and friend was lost,
The mark was missed, but mortal man wasn't,
When a bloody battle-shaft caused brotherly grief.
A fearful arrow-flight, and a fatal sorrow,
Heartache for Hrethel, and harder still than that,

No payment in blood for the prince's death, no penalty exacted.
It was as the bitterness borne by a bent old man
When his son has to swing on the sorrowful gallows,
Riding high for the ravens. A wretched end,
With a sorrowful song for the son left there hanging,
The ravens' repast—no rescue possible · 2450
From an elderly, impotent, and aching old man.
Always alone, every morning, he enters every day,
Knowing the heir is elsewhere gone, an empty hall left,
All is desolate, he has no desire to delve in the future,
Waiting to bequeath his wealth to a ward newborn,
Now that death's dominion devastated his house.
Miserable man! He musters the courage to look
On the lodge of his lost son, the last place of his happiness,
Bereft now of rejoicing. The rider now sleeps,
That hero, hidden away in death. Harps no longer play, 2460
In the courtyards no clear songs, as the custom once was.

Thirty-Fifth Fitt † *Beowulf reminisces, challenges dragon, thanes flee*

He greets the gulf in his chamber, a grief song is lifted,
His loss is too large for him. Too large also all else,
His hall and his hearth. So the high king of the Weders
Carried heavy care in his collapsed heart for Herebeald,
Wave after wave of woe unrelenting.
Vengeance was averted by the voice of conscience—
He could not slay his son, or say words of harassment
For that foul and fatal mistake, though he favored him no more.
For all the sorrow his soul went through, that seared him through, 2470
He gave up all gladness and God's light chose.
Buildings and all blessings he bequeathed to his sons,
As a prosperous prince would do when passing from earth.

There was struggling and strife between the Swedes and Geats
Over wide waterways—the warfare was constant,
Hardscrabble and hand-to-hand, after Hrethel had died,
For Ongentheow's offspring were still eager for battle,
Settled on strife and seeking a fight.
They had no passion for peace, but pummeled their way
2480 In hatred of their hosts near Hreosnabeorh.
My family and friends fought a feud for just vengeance,
Not for spite nor malice, as is known by all,
Though one of their warriors won it with blood;
A bargain of bitterness, for the boldness of Haethcyn
Proved fatal in that fight for the first of the Geats.
With morning as herald, I heard the head of the killer struck,
And the clansman was conquered with a clean stroke.
When Ongentheow eagerly sought Eofor in battle.
That war-helm split wide, and pale white he fell down,
2490 That wise Scylfing warrior. The wild hand that struck
Remembered all death debts and dealt the blow.
For the gifts he gave me, my grip on the sword
Repaid him in plenty with the power I brought.
I had lordly gifts and lands, laden with his generosity,
I had a hearth and hall. He hardly needed
Swedish mercenaries or men, or more help from Spear-Danes,
Or gift-help from the Gifthas to gather support,
Or some worse warriors who need *wages* to fight!
I fought in the front and fiercely delivered,
2500 Standing steadfast, and so I always fight
While my blade proves bold and my bravery lasts,
As it has repeatedly proven—profoundly loyal—
Since I dealt out death and Dayraven died,
Felled by my fisted might, that Frankish champion.
He brought no booty back to the bold king of the Frisians,

Whether baubles or breast gems, or bedazzling gold work.
Rather, slain in that slaughter, that standard-bearer fell,
The pride of princes. A pointed sword didn't do it,
But his breast bone was shattered and broken by hand,
His heartbeat halted. The hilted sword now,   2510
Hard edge in my hand, over hoard-gold will battle."
Bold Beowulf spoke, and his brave words were clear,
His finest and final words: "I have fought many wars
In my younger years—now yearning for honor,
A tested and true defender, triumph I seek,
Doing deeds of great daring, if that dragon of fire
Comes from his cavern as I call him to battle!"
Then that great king greeted his good men for the last time,
That high-helmeted warrior hailed each of them there,
With dear words of devotion. "I would dare this weaponless,   2520
No sword for this serpent, if I saw it as humble—
Fighting such a foe with fantastic vows,
And a grip on his great throat as with Grendel I prevailed.
But here—burning breath and blasts from his nostrils,
And powerful poison, so prepared I have come
With buckler and breastplate. And I won't back away
One step from my station. I will stand to the end
In our war near the wall, as wyrd may allow,
That master of men. My mind is eager
But I am bound to not boast over this battle-flyer.   2530
Now near this barrow abide in your bold armor,
You high-hearted heroes, and hold yourselves back—
You will see soon enough who suffers the worst of it.
Wait out our warfare. This wasting fight
Is for me to make happen, my mettle to measure,
My might with this monster, my mind to keep strong
With high-hearted heroics. Hard battle awaits,

And I will win through to wealth or wake up in heaven,
Killed by that cruel one, your kind king and leader."
2540 Fierce in his fearsome helmet that fighting champion stood,
Trusting in his tested strength, and his last trial faced.
With his blade and buckler he bent low and entered
Under the craggy cliffs—no coward that one!
Soon enough the king saw smoke from that fire—
That survivor of sure victories, and certain in bravery,
From fields of fighting, when furious men clashed—
Along the reach of the rampart, from the rocky stone arch,
A brook from that barrow with burning hot water,
Above it fire flashing, forbidding any approach.
2550 To hold ground there was hopeless, hot harm was waiting,
Dark pain enduring from the dragon fire.
Then Beowulf burst out, rage blasting in a roar,
His shout was not shallow, a sure cry from the Geat leader,
Sturdy in heart, he stormed, and struck with his voice,
His cry was courageous, clear, beneath cliffs of deep gray.
The dragon in the deep heard human danger approach,
And his rage unwrapped, erupting in violence,
No pact of peace here. That pestilent worm
Came out of the cave to conquer a man,
2560 Eager in his anger, the ancient rocks shook.
Standing by the stone door, his sturdy shield raised,
The bold lord Beowulf braved the onslaught,
While that coiled cruelty with cold courage
Was flared for the fight. The fell king
Drew sword from his scabbard, summoning bravery,
With that ancient heirloom. Each of them faced off
With an awesome adversary in an angered high mettle.
Stout, standing fast, he stopped with his shield up,
That leader and lord, as the loathsome worm coiled

In serpentine spirals. The splendid king waited.   2570
Now unwinding in wickedness the worm darted forward,
Fiery and fierce. The firm shield held fast,
Body and soul safely, but not so long
As the desire of the dauntless one decided was needed.
The respite he required was rejected
In his warfare this once. So wyrd would not have it,
While the high prince held firm and hewed with his blade,
The lord and leader of Geats, that loathsome foe struck
With his ancient heirloom, but that edge turned aside—
The bone bent the blade, and his blow was feebler   2580
Than that high-hearted hero had need of then,
Harassed and harried as he was. Then the hoard-monster
Swelled in riotous rage in wrath for that blow,
Firing his flames, fierce in his anger.
Victory was a vain hope; the vicious breath flared,
And the Weder lord was weary; his wasted blade failed,
Futile for fighting, and that for the first time—
It was a great and good blade. Grim and not easy
Was the path of Ecgtheow's heir, answering fate,
As he left home and hall, a home far off to seek,   2590
Gone from the good earth to gain his everlasting hall,
As all men must, leaving middle-earth behind,
And their leasehold on life—not long after
Those combatants closed again, and clashed in fury.
That hoard-guard took heart, exhaling heat and fire,
Swelled up with a second wind, and the struggle was joined again,
And Beowulf was in the blaze, that brave ruler of Geats.
His comrades lost courage, his comrades all bolted,
Born of nobles, they bolted, all bested by fear.
They wavered in warfare, to the woods they all fled,   2600
To save their sorry lives. One single retainer

Felt the sorrows of sympathy—that sign of true kinship
Will not wester or waver in a *worthy* mind.

THIRTY-SIXTH FITT † *Wiglaf's speech, rally, Beowulf wounded*

Weohstan's son, Wiglaf, was that wise thane remaining,
A solid shield-bearer, a Scylfing prince,
Kinsman or cousin to Aelfhere. His king he saw struggling,
His helmet heated terribly, the fight going hard for him.
He brought to mind memories, the marvels his lord had gifted him,
Wealthy holdings, wide halls for the Waegmunding tribe,
2610 Keeps and common lands that were kept by his father.
It was too hard to hold back. He held up his yellow linden shield,
He seized his great sword, from the scabbard he drew it—
Eanmund, son of Ohthere, had that heirloom at first,
And he was slain in some slaughter, struck down by Weohstan,
Friendless in futile exile, he fought and he lost.
So Weohstan won for his kin the war gear of Eanmund,
A bright, burnished helmet, a breastplate of woven rings,
A grip hilt for giants, all given to Onela,
Who, tested, returned them, which told of his mercy;
2620 He knew that his nephew was the noble who fell,
But he refused the feud, and favored Weohstan.
For many winters Weohstan kept it, this war-gear he won,
Chain mail and choice shield, till his chosen son was grown,
And wrought feats like his father, and could fight his own battles.
So he gave him that gear—with the Geats they lived then—
A huge collection he had conquered, when he counted out his days,
As old men always do. Now that eager young warrior,
With his lord and leader, was a lieutenant strong,
And was called to combat, the collision of true battle.
2630 His war-wisdom did not waver, nor was the wish of his lord

Denied in that defense, as the drake soon found out
When those foes finally fought and finished the matter.
Wiglaf spoke wisely, and his words were fitting,
As he, grieved and grim, said gravely to his comrades,
"My mind full remembers, when mead was given to us,
And the proud hall-promises that our prince heard from us.
He gave us rings; we were resolute, we refused to dishonor him.
We promised our pride, we professed our deep loyalty.
For helmets and hard edges, we held out allegiance
For strife of this sort. And so he selected us   2640
From his entire army to enlist with him here.
He called us companions, covered us with gifts,
Considering and counting us to have courage with the spear,
To be good in grim battle, and grave in our helmets.
Our courageous king had counted on being alone,
Our fighting folk-king wanted to finish alone,
He has gathered glory, great among men
For deeds of great daring. But the day is upon us
When our lord and leader needs lieutenants, stout-hearted.
Bring our strength, let us *stand* with him! Let us strike at the dragon;   2650
Let us help our hero-king while the heat is upon him,
Fiery and fierce. For God is witness
I would fare far better if the fire took me
Together with our good king, a gift of honorable death.
It would hardly be right—a horror—if hanging our heads,
We carried craven shields home, cowards all of us,
Instead of standing firm and struggling to save
The life of our Weder lord. The laws of honor
Forbid our bold king to brave it alone,
To be the good Geat warrior who gave us his strength,   2660
And sank in the strife. This sword and this helmet,
Breastplate, bold shield will be better for both of us."

Through the furious fumes he fought his way forward,
Bringing his battle-helmet, and briefly said,
"Beowulf, dear and dauntless, do what you do,
As when young, yearning for glory, you vowed great things,
Saying you would not waver, and that while life was in you,
Your glory would not go. Now, great in heroics,
Prince of high prowess, protect your life
2670 With all your stated strength. I will stand here with you."
At those daring, dauntless words, the dragon came again,
Eager and angry, and with envious rage,
Uncoiling in cruelty, its courageous hated ones to seek,
The fire unfurled, the flames came in waves
And burned down to the boss, the breastplate also failed
To protect the young prince who, empowered with courage,
Went quickly under his kinsman's shield, keeping faith,
Since his own emblem was eaten by fire,
All burned to blazes. The brave king again
2680 Called to mind and memory the might of his glory,
Thrust his striking sword at the serpent's head,
A blow of blunt hatred. But the blade, Naegling, shattered,
Beowulf's sword broke, in battle it staggered,
Old and gray-ancient. The edge of the sword
Was fated to fail him; faltering at great moments
Of struggle and strife. So strong was his hand,
As the tale was told me, he tested them hard,
And with the strength of each stroke he struck them to pieces—
All the blades he would break, and was no better off.
2690 Then the dread fire-dragon determined to end it
And rushed in his rage to wreak final vengeance.
He found an opening finally and furiously bit
With his fangs in a fury, and fastened them deep
In the neck of that noble, in the neck of the hero—
In waves his blood welled, and he weltered in crimson.

I have heard the high courage, how the great hero, Wiglaf,
Helped his king with his courage, and kept his high honor,
With deeds of great daring and deep honor of nature.
He did not hit at the head, his hand badly burned,
High-hearted, heroic, he helped his great king.   2700
He lunged and struck lower and the loathsome drake
Was struck with that steel; his sword pierced the neck,
A bright, bitter blade, the blaze of the dragon
Diminished and dimmed. A desperate stroke
Came from the king, as he cut with his knife,
A blade from his belt, by his breastplate kept,
That great Weder warrior wounded his belly,
Cut him, killed him, and conquered the dragon.
Kinsmen together killed it, conquerors both of them.
That's what a thane should be!—His first thought for valor   2710
In day of great danger. That daring accomplishment
Was the king's last conquest, his last captured glory,
His final work in the world. The wound festered immediately,
What that earth-drake inflicted in his eager malice.
The wound seethed and swelled; soon Beowulf knew
That his breast was burning, blood-venomous poison,
The pain of deep poison. The prince staggered across,
Still wise in his wisdom, to the wall straight across.
He sat and stared at the stonework of giants,
Those proud arches and pillars, piled high in wisdom,   2720
Upholding the hall that held the great dragon.
Then the hand of the hero, the high-hearted Wiglaf,
Brought blessed water his brave lord to cool,
Clotted and covered with conquering blood.
His struggle ceasing, he unstrapped his helmet.

Bold Beowulf spoke brief words through his hurt,
His fatal wound that felled him. He full well knew
His joy was justly departing; he was joining his fathers,
He had finished his long file of fleeting days,
2730 His day of doom upon him, his death was approaching.
"I would give gifts to a good son of mine—
All these garments, this gear, I would gladly bestow
If I had a high prince who could inherit my name.
As a prince of this people I provided just rule,
Fifty winters of favor. No fierce invader,
None, not one, from nations nearby
Would wage war on me, working their mischief,
Or proud provocations. At peace, I stayed home
And welcomed the waiting respite, and I worked no intrigues;
2740 I fought no senseless feuds and was false in no oaths.
Though a man mortally wounded, I marvel at goodness—
No blood-guilt besmirches me, and blessed I am.
Mankind's Ruler restores me, no wrath rests upon me—
As my life is leaving me, and losses prevail—
For the killing of kin. Quickly, now go
To take in that treasure tucked under gray stone,
Bold, beloved Wiglaf, now that beast lies sleeping,
Cold in his cruelty, cut off from his treasure.
Go, gather in haste. I would get a good look
2750 At the golden glory, the gorgeous treasures,
Take in joy through the gems, rejoice in my dying,
Made better, not bitter, as I bestow an inheritance
Of my life and legacy and the length of my rule."

Thirty-Eighth Fitt † *Beowulf sees the treasure, orders his burial*

I don't wonder at this word, that Weohstan's son
Took the words and wishes of his wounded king,

And went, although weary, in his woven chain mail,
Bent into the barrow, and bravely went in.
Passing the supreme seat, he saw a vast treasure,
That young kinsman of courage, caught a glimpse of great heaps
Of glistering gold and gems on the floor. 2760
The wall tapestries were a wonder, wrought with great cunning,
In the den of that drake, that ancient dawn-flier,
Unburnished beakers that brave men once held,
Bereft of their richness; rusty helmets scattered.
Scores of torques in the treasure told of their craftsmanship.
Such wealth can rob wisdom, steal wit from mankind,
Might overcome anyone, all men are vulnerable,
However you hide it—heed this fair warning!
Then he glimpsed a gold standard, great splendor giving,
Above the hoard hanging, handcraft of wise women, 2770
Embroidered and bright, a brilliant light came from it,
So he took in the treasure floor, and tasted the wealth,
Viewing their victory. That cruel victim was dead,
No sign of the serpent; their swords had dispatched him.
So, that hill I have heard had its hoard pillaged,
Great gifts from the earth, what giants had wrought.
One man made his way out, with many a wonder,
With gold cups, with gold dishes, and the gold standard,
Bright in its brilliance. His brave lord's sword,
Edged with hard iron, had entered the vitals 2780
Of the great and grim sentry of the golden pile,
Who time out of mind, terrible, that tyrant of greed,
Blew hot and horror, and held safe his treasure,
Until he died, desolate, in the dead of the night.
Then this high-hearted hero, that hoard left behind,
Retracing his true path, tried in his soul,
As to whether the Weder king, wounded and bleeding,

Would still be lingering alive where he had left him above,
Weakening, wounded, by the wall of gray rock.
2790 So he took out the treasure and took in the king,
Still bleeding, still brave, that bold and great chieftain,
Still losing his lifeblood. Again the lieutenant
Wet his forehead with water—a word finally came out,
Broke from his breast-treasury. Beowulf spoke,
Ancient, elder king, as he eyed all the gold,
"For the gleaming gold here, the great God I thank,
To that worker of wonders, my words are lifted
To Heaven's high Lord, behold, all the treasure!
By the grace of God I give this treasure,
2800 On the day of my death, for a deserving, good people.
My final breath is bartered, a bargain I call it,
To gain all this gold. Give yourself to the task,
Care for the commonwealth. I can tarry no longer.
Build me a barrow, with all my battle friends,
When the pyre's heat is past, on the proud headland,
At the wide Whale Cliff, a witness to glory,
A memorial for men, my memory to keep,
So crews under sail coming by may call it by name,
Calling it Beowulf's barrow, as breezing homeward,
2810 They work their white-throated ships over the wine dark sea."
Then the good king unclasped his great collar of gold,
Gave it with thanks to his thane, with thought to be generous,
Gave his helmet and hard breastplate, and he held out his ring,
And bade him receive with boldness, and with a blessing to use them.
"You are the last living man who is left of our race,
The way of the Waegmundings. Wyrd has taken us all,
All my clan has been conquered and, kept in their doom,
Great earls in their glory. I must go to them now."
This word from that warrior was wisdom at last,

What he wished to say before the waves of heat
From his calling pyre consumed him. From that courageous heart
His soul was sent out, a saint's reward to find.

Thirty-Ninth Fitt † *Wiglaf rebukes the cowardly thanes*

It was a hard hit—the young hero was staggered
To look down on his lord, laid out on the earth
With the great, grievous wound that got him his end.
But the dragon was dead and done with predation,
That earth-dragon, evil night-flier, eager in cruelty,
Brave blows struck him dead, bold were his killers.
That coiled cruelty was done, and could not keep his treasure.
Iron with hard edges had ended his life,
Brilliant and battle-sharp, the blunt hammers' labor,
Had felled that high flier, his flames were all quenched,
Silenced in that slaughter, its death summons final.
No longer aloft at midnight, circling left and then right,
Boasting in his blazes, making brave men quake,
Proud of its prowess, prideful in wealth,
It felled the hand of that high-hearted man, the hero and king.
There are hardly any heroes who could hold their own,
Though stout and steadfast, as the scops all sing,
With such a poisonous serpent, against such odds—
The poisonous breath of that pestilence, the power of that worm,
Who might dare that deep cave, and delve into the rings,
When that watchful worm was still awake and alive.
Beowulf was bold, and at the barrow he died.
The price of life was precious, precious treasure indeed,
And both man and monster met their end at last,
The end of all days. After a while
The cowards crept back to the cave and to Wiglaf,

Oath-breakers, all of them, ashamed in their cowardice,
2850 Ten who were tried and tempted to fear,
At their lord's final limit, they left with their spears.
In shame, their shields lowered, they shuffled back,
In their metal mail-shirts, where their manly leader rested,
And looked at war-weary Wiglaf. Watching his king,
He sat by the shoulder, a stout-hearted thane,
Still washing him with water, whether it did good or not.
However deeply devoted he was, this death took his king away,
And he could not keep life in his courageous king's body,
Or ward off the will of the only wise God.
2860 The Word that works all things is the word of the Lord
For all men, and every man, as He always does.
Hard words with hard edges were hot and came easily,
From that courageous young courtier to cowards standing there.
Wiglaf spoke wisely, Weohstan's son,
A grieved and good man, to those who had gone running,
"To tell all the truth, this tale is easy enough—
This ring-giving ruler who richly rewarded you
With battle gear, bucklers, and hilts embossed well,
Whose mind would remember his mead-bench retainers
2870 And in his hall would give helmets and well-hardened breastplates,
As lord to lieutenants, the loveliest weapons
Whether far off he found them, or found them at home,
They were wasted on *these* warriors, weapons just thrown away,
Given to men who gave no battle, who would rather grovel than fight.
Our bold king could not boast of brave comrades in arms,
But the Ruler of victory, the Righteous One, gave revenge to his arm.
God gave him great strength and grace for battle,
So that with solitary sword in the strife he prevailed.
To assist in that struggle, to save his life,
2880 There was little or less my lord could expect from me,

But I managed to maim the drake, but little more to help my king.
Its energy ebbed, the eager fire dimmed
When I struck with my sword that beast was slower than he was.
When manly courage should remain, you men were off in the woods,
In throes of thick battle, you thought to run off.
Now the giving of gifts and the goods of exchanging,
The joys of hall and hearth, and all home-delights,
Shall fade from families, your freeholds taken,
Your clansman and kinfolk will be caught up in exile,
When distant nobles deny that such a deed should be ignored,   2890
Hearing of your feckless flight, inflamed with indignation.
No, death is a good deal better than deserting your king,
Which for a lord's lieutenant is a life of shame."

FORTIETH FITT † *Wiglaf expects trouble and broods*

Then he calmly commanded that the conquest be announced
To those retainers on the ridge who had rested in sorrow
All that morning, meditating; men of nobility,
Holding shields, shaking their heads, summoning doubts.
Would they welcome their lord home or bewail his loss?
The herald sent held nothing back, though it hurt to announce.
The tidings were told, and the tale was full,   2900
By the herald who rode up the headland and held forth.
"Now the wise ruler of Weders, who willingly gave gifts,
On his deathbed lies dedicated, that great defender of Geats,
He sleeps fast, slaughtered by the serpent's malice.
Beside him, that man-slaying monster remembers nothing,
Done in by dagger strokes, this was not done with swords,
No blow from a long blade sliced the beast open.
So Wiglaf, Weohstan's son, sat wondering
By the brave-hearted Beowulf, beside his dead lord,

2910 A still-living leader beside a lord who died valiantly,
And a heart-heavy watch by two heads keeps vigil,
Over dead friend and dead foe, both dead together.
Our people must prepare themselves, prepare for battle—
When the Frisians and Franks hear of the fall of our king,
When that message makes its way across many lands.
Remember how Hygelac harried his enemies,
Taking his fleet to the Frisians, and fled from them there.
The Hetware humbled him, hitting him hard in battle,
Avenging the wrong with vaster force, victory was easily theirs,
2920 And our bold battle-leader was bent beneath them,
Falling in the fighting. No more favor in ring-giving
From that faithful leader and lord. And from that time
The Merovingian men brought their malice against us.
Nor do I expect eagerness for accepting peace
From the Swedes and some others. It was said far and wide
That the anger of Ongentheow attacked his enemy's life,
Haethcyn, son of Hrethel, who lost hope and life at Ravenswood,
When Geats in great pride sought glory in battle against
The best of the Battle-Scylfings. Soon the boldness of Ohthere,
2930 Aged but eager, old but cunning,
Struck back with a blow, and beat the sea-king,
Killing him coldly, and his queen taking back.
He rescued that rich wife, though bereft of her wealth,
Mother of Ohtere and Onela, aged queen.
Then he hunted his hostile foes, his hated enemy,
Sore pressed and pressured, he pursued them hotly,
They barely made it back, beating their retreat to Ravenswood.
With his high-hearted host, he held siege for the survivors.
The wound-weary men, wretched, had made it to refuge.
2940 But all night he angered them by attacking with words, saying,
In the morning some men would be mown down by swords,

And some would swing on the sullen gallows-tree,
As ravens' delight, ravenous birds. But rescue was timely
When the day dawned for those despairing men
And they heard the great horn of Hygelac's company,
The free timbre of his trumpet; with troops behind him,
Their loyal leader led men to the rescue.

FORTY-FIRST FITT † *Hygelac kills Ongentheow, the Swedes will be back*

"There was a swath of Swedes, a bloody swath of Geats,
A trail of blood and trial, talked about everywhere,
How those two tribes tore into each other.   2950
Then the aged Ongentheow, eager for respite,
Sought out a stronghold, foreseeing great trouble.
So he sought out a citadel, seeking his refuge.
He knew Hygelac was hale and a hard man in battle,
He knew his pride and his prowess, a powerful fighter,
So he sought out safety from those sea-wandering fighters.
The king had no confidence he could keep his great treasure,
His kingly sons and his queen, so he quit him again,
Aged one, to his earthwall. Hot after him came
The high banners of Hygelac that were held over the field,   2960
With the battle plain bloodied, and the Geats had the better of it
Till the brave and bold Hrethelings breached the walls of the town.
Ongentheow, battling boldly, was brought to bay,
Grim and gray-headed, he gripped his sword fiercely,
And fought Eofor's fury, that fighting king was backed against it.
Against his enemy's anger, who attacked the king.
Wulf, Wonred's son, swung his weapon hard,
And blood spurted in streams, surging from beneath his hair.
But the sturdy old Scylfing stood firmly without fear,
And a blow came straight back with a blade of vengeance.   2970

Wulf got the worst of it as their weapons flew,
And he faced his foe with fierce intentions.
Wonred's son was not swift enough as he summoned his answer
To deliver with daring to that doughty king.
He took a hit to the head; his helmet was split—
He bent toward earth, bloodied, as bravely he fell.
The blow was deadly, he fell down, but his doom was not yet,
That edge entered him deep, but he after recovered.
Then Eofer the fierce, a fighting thane for Hygelac,
2980 When his bold brother fell, swung his blade in anger,
An old, ancient giant blade that entered great helmets,
Over the shield wall, he shattered the helmet and shuttered that king.
The old shepherd fell, fatally struck, forever fallen,
He left his aged life, at the last fell to the ground.
The brother's wounds were bound; they brought him up,
Raised him upright, righting him when there was space
For them to keep and control what they had conquered in war.
Eofor took off Ongentheow the iron breastplate,
Warrior from warrior, taking weapons also,
2990 Hilted sword and helmet, a hard edge captured.
He took them heroically to Hygelac, holding the grayhead's armor,
Who received them royally and registered his promises
To reward them handsomely at home, and held his word firmly.
For great deeds in grim battle, the Geat lord was generous,
High-hearted, son of Hrethel, when home was theirs,
To warriors Eofor and Wulf gave a wealth of great riches,
One hundred thousand high honors in hearth-land and rings.
No man resented the riches, it was reckoned well worth it,
As these men were mighty, marvelous in battle.
3000 And Eofor he honored, eagerly gave his one daughter,
The grace of his great house, the gift of his home.
This is the feud I fear, the ferocity of tribes,

When the Swedes are summoned by our sorrowful loss,
And come in their cruelty, seeking conquest and pillage,
For this fatal fight of theirs, the fell-Scylfings,
When they learn of our loss, that our lord lies dead,
Who led us in life, and gave lands and treasures,
And defended them fighting from our foes and enemies.
He fell, his life's clasp fastened, he finished his race
A hero high-hearted. Let us hasten now,   3010
As we gaze on our Geat lord, as we go to mourn him,
And carry the king, who collected rings for giving,
To the bier we have built for Beowulf our lord.
No small bits shall burn with his bones together.
Great gems and gold, glittering jewels without number,
A treasure torn free by that trial taking his life.
The blaze will take the booty, let the burning fire eat it.
No warrior can willingly carry the work-craft found here.
No lady of loveliness will light up her radiance
With a tempting torque for the neck, twisted in gold.   3020
No, she will never walk at home, but benighted in exile,
With her gladness gone, gold stolen, she will walk alone,
Just as our lifeless leader has lost all his joys,
All lightness and laughter. Many a lifted spear
Shall greet the grim cold mornings, shall be gripped for battle,
And hefted in scarred hands; no harp will play
To wake the warriors. But the wan-dark raven
Feasts on the fallen, with puffed feathers he boasts
To the enticed eagle how he ate without measure,
As raven and ravening wolf were rending the bodies."   3030
So the herald held forth with hurting words;
He did not deceive, his deed was true.
Weary in heart, the warriors rose and wound their way,
Mourning, they made their way, up the mound to Eagle Cliff.

The men all went, weeping, the wonder to see.
They found him still, on the sand, stretched out in death,
Their leader, now lifeless, he who had lavished gold
On heroes in happier days. His halting day had come,
It had dawned on this daring one; death had come to the king,
3040 A good and great king, and a glorious death.
Beside the king was the conquered worm, his cruelty ceased,
Lying next to their lord, still loathsome in death,
His scales scorched, this serpent of fire,
Laid out like lumber, his light and fire gone.
It was fifty feet long, the full measure of hate,
Laid out grim on the ground. Its glory was night-flying,
Seeking its den only at dawn, But death had him now,
Held firm forever in the fist of cold death.
He lost his lease on that low earth hall.
3050 Scattered and strewn about were stacks of bowls, cups,
Dishes with inlaid decorations, and jewel bedecked swords,
Wrecked and rust-bitten, resting on the lap of the earth,
Waiting a thousand winters, wasting away.
For that large legacy, that left behind gold,
By ancient, honorable men, was edged with a spell,
Leaving the treasure untouchable, temptation out of reach,
For any humble human soul, unless Heaven's Ruler,
The great God Himself, might give it away,
As Protector of princes, the priceless hoard to bestow
3060 To such a man as seemed most suitable to him.

Forty-Second Fitt † *Cursed treasure examined*

It proved perilous indeed for the poor soul who came
To hide in that hall, hiding from justice.
Its guardian was grim and got his revenge.

In cruelty he killed one of us, and the king retaliated,
But that deed was dire. Dread wonder strikes—
How might a man of magnificent strength
Come to life's limit, when that lord no longer
May laugh in the mead-hall with merry friends.
So Beowulf, that brave one, when the barrow-guard he fought,
A conflict deeply contested, he could not know   3070
In what manner of men he should leave middle-earth at last.
Princes their curses pronounced, those who put the gold there,
And damned until doomsday the desperate fool
So that man might be marked with measurements for sin,
Held with hell-chains, and horrors plenty,
Torments testing him, who should take from that hoard.
That gracious king was not greedy, but the grace of heaven
Was what the king in his kindness had kept in mind.
Wiglaf, son of Weohstan, spoke words from the heart,
"One destiny for warriors, as wisdom shows us,   3080
Is suffering and sorrow, and so we submit to it.
Our courageous king our counsel rejected,
Our beloved lord left our petitions aside.
That guardian of greed should have gone unmolested,
Should have been left alone, lying in that lair of sin,
Kept in that cold cavern till the climax of the world,
But he held to his high course, and the hoard is now ours,
Though we paid a precious price; that penalty is grievous
For the task which took our tale-rich king and lord.
I went down to that weird chamber where I saw the gold,   3090
Mounds of magnificent treasure, when the moment was given me,
A gift not easily granted, to go down there,
Under the earth-fortress. With bold eagerness, I seized
As much from those mounds as a man can carry,
And hurried back in haste to my high prince,

My lord and leader . . . alive he still was,
Waiting in wise patience, his wit still active.
In sorrow he spoke, and said to greet you.
He said to build him a bier when his breath was gone,
3100 Where we burn his bones, the barrow should be high,
A magnificent memorial, massive and worthy of him.
He was the best of the brave ones, the boldest of men,
During his days, when he dealt out rings.
Let us go down the great hole a grim second time
And search out these stores of silver and gold,
Wondrous delights, strange devices, down we will go,
Where you may gaze at the gold, glimpsing splendor,
Bracelets and brave jewels. Let the bier be fashioned now,
Ready to roar when we return to the surface.
3110 We must carry our king, our courageous prince—
Beloved lord!—where the long days begin,
Safe from all sorrow in the shelter—God's keeping."
Then Wiglaf, son of Weohstan, gave words of command
To his fierce fighters, to his faithful men
Who owned their own lands, to urgently bring
Wood to feed the fire; the flames would be hungry
At the funeral of that famous king. "Now fire shall eat,
And dark flames devour our devoted leader,
Who would stand steadfast when struggle was joined,
3120 Under the arch of arrows when anger loosed them,
And they came cunningly; keeping the shaft
And the flocked feathers and the fatal head all together."
The son of Weohstan, full of sense, said he would choose
Seven wise warriors. Wizened and great-hearted,
The bravest and best formed the band to descend.
He, the eighth warrior, eagerly led; the entrance swallowed them.
He held a lit torch aloft and led the way down

Under the evil roof of that iniquitous hall.
No lots were allowed for the looting privilege;
They saw in a moment how much there was, how many piles,   3130
With no serpent for a sentry, and all scattered about.
They lost little time, leaving nothing behind,
And they hauled it out with heavy loads and heavy hearts.
The deadly treasure cost them dear. The dragon they dragged
To the cold cliff-edge, committing it to water,
The surf swallowed him, a now silent carcass.
Then torques and entwined gold pieces were tossed into wagons,
Riches beyond reckoning. The royal one was carried,
Kingly, in quiet majesty, to the Cape of Whales.

FORTY-THIRD FITT † *Funeral of Beowulf, no hope*

Then the Geats in their grief, having gathered the wood,   3140
Assembled an impressive pyre and piled treasure on it.
Helmets were hanging there, harnesses and shields,
Breastplates burnished, as he had bidden them.
In the midst they laid their marvelous king, mighty prince,
Great heroes grieving their good master gone.
Then for the king they kindled a colossal blaze,
Clouds of smoke curled upward, closing the sky,
Black smoke, blaze red, and blending in sorrow
Was the crackling fire and keening people—quiet was the wind—
Until the body burst and the bones were blackened   3150
By the great heat at the heart of it. With hurting spirits,
They grieved in great sorrow at their good lord's passing.
An old Weder widow wailed in grief,
Her hair coiled for the king, a keening prophetess,
She sang sorrowfully and said what she feared.
She dreaded doom of battle, the days to come

Would be devastating, deadly, dark, and shameful.
There would be sorrow and sadness. The sky drank the smoke.
The Weder-Geats worked and when done,
3160 There was a barrow on the bluff, broad and high,
Easily seen by seafarers, those sent from afar.
It took them ten days, and the tomb was prepared
For the brave battle-king. They built walls for his ashes,
The ramparts of royalty, a righteous tribute,
The best they could build with their better artisans.
They brought to the barrow the booty, that treasure,
All the baubles and bracelets that had been brought before
From that hoard by heroes, by hostiles or friends.
They gave to the ground a great treasure indeed,
3170 Gold in the ground, a gift to the silence,
As useless now as it used to be, as useless now as it ever was.
Then around that barrow brave men rode, battle-tested,
Champions, chieftains, twelve children of princes,
To lament their lost king, to lift their respect,
To keen their cold dirge, to collect their honor.
They praised his princely rule, his power and kindness;
They deemed him devoted. They did well.
Men should praise masters when masters do well,
And hold up high praise when they have to depart
3180 From this life of loss to the life everlasting.
Thus the Geats grieved and gave a great mourning
For the loss of their leader, kind lord and ring-giver.
A captain of kings, they called him beloved,
Of men the mildest, and most respected,
Kind to his clansmen, and keen for true honor.

ESSAYS

Beowulf: The UnChrist

The poetry of *Beowulf* is not just an artistic triumph, although it certainly is that. As the themes of *Beowulf* are carefully considered and weighed, it should also be considered as an evangelistic and apologetic *tour de force*.[8]

Both the pagan and Christian elements in the poem are obvious and readily visible, and much scholarly debate has raged over the relationship between them and what to do about the tension that these two elements create for one another in the poem. Usually the sides choose up according to whether they believe the paganism is fundamental to the worldview of the poem, with Christian elements sprinkled on top, or whether the Christian elements are fundamental, with the paganism (inexplicably) sprinkled on top. In both cases, the tension is frequently treated as an accidental by-product of poetic incompetence or inadequate redaction of two or more different sources.

I want to argue here that the two elements were placed in tension by the poet deliberately, and that he did this in order to accomplish a stunning apologetic for the Christian faith. The result is a powerful *praeparatio ad conversionem*. The *Beowulf* poet is not syncretistic in his inclinations at all. He is not like one of those backsliding monks at Lindisfarne, sternly rebuked by Alcuin for paying attention to the ancient heroic tales:

---

8. This essay appeared in a shorter form some years ago in *Touchstone* magazine. That shorter form can be accessed here: http://www.touchstonemag.com/archives/article.php?id=20-06-030-f.

"What has Ingeld to do with Christ? The house is narrow, it cannot contain both. The king of the heavens will have nothing to do with heathen and damned so-called kings. For the eternal king rules in the heavens, the lost heathen repines in hell."[9]

But our poet is not a conflicted monk at that particular *minster*, reading James Joyce under the covers at night with a flashlight. The paganism that is so evident throughout this poem is presented to us by a thoroughly Christian poet, and he does not show us this paganism in order to say, "See, pagans can be noble, too—even without Jesus!" Rather, he is doing precisely the opposite—he is refusing to engage in a fight with a heathen straw man of his own devising. He acknowledges the high nobility that was there, but then he bluntly shows us that nobility *at the point of profound despair*. The effect is extremely potent. Instead of saying that nobility is possible without Christ, the poet is showing that without Christ, such nobility does not keep a people from being utterly and completely *lost*. To adapt a comment made by C. S. Lewis about Homer, the gray granite of pagan nobility in the poem is polished to shine like marble, but it is still granite for all that. This is nobility at the end of its tether.

In this approach the poet is taking his cue from the apostle Paul. When St. Paul attacks the "natural man" (1 Corinthians 2:14) he is *not* taking on all the drug addicts, winos, and hookers of Corinth. Rather, he is referring to man at his best—yachtsman, advisor to kings and presidents, philosopher, harpsichord player, and war hero. *That* was the man who did not "know God" (1 Corinthians 1:21). St. Paul was taking on the Corinthian aristocracy, and something very similar is happening here.

The *Beowulf* poet is not seeking to praise paganism in order to make any room for it. His task is far more profound. Paganism

---

9. As quoted in Paul Cavill, *Anglo-Saxon Christianity* (London: HarperCollins, 1999), 57. It is most interesting (at least to me) that Alcuin mentions Ingeld here, a minor character in *Beowulf*.

at its best, at its *most* noble and heroic, was still without hope and without God in the world. If paganism at its best and most aristocratic was a really fine car, the *Beowulf* poet climbs into it and drives it into a tree.

The action of the poem is on both sides of AD 521, taking this hard date from Gregory of Tours's mention of Hygelac's disastrous raid on the Frisians. The conversion of the Anglo-Saxons to the Christian faith began in earnest about seventy years later, in the 590s. "During three or four generations starting in the 590s, all the English kings and their courts converted to Christianity."[10] Not only so, but we also know from history that both the Danes and the Geats (if they existed) were unconverted pagans at the time of Hygelac.[11]

If we place the *Beowulf* poet in the early eighth century, this is just one century after the Anglo-Saxons began this process and only about fifty years after it was generally concluded. "By 660 only the men of Sussex and the Isle of Wight remained pagan, and soon they too were converted."[12] This is just one generation. To place it in an analogous context, my father-in-law was wounded in the battle of Guadalcanal in the Second World War. I am a fifty-year-old man,[13] easily able to visit with him about the details of that battle, a battle that was sixty-one years before. In short, the *Beowulf* poet could easily have known individual Christian Anglo-Saxons who had converted from paganism. In fact, the poet's own parents could easily have been in that position. That world was dead and gone, but it was not necessarily "long ago and far away."

So their conversion from paganism was not "old news" for them. Paganism was still the faith of numerous other European tribes and peoples, and the time of Anglo-Saxon paganism was still within

10. John Blair, *The Anglo-Saxon Age* (Oxford: Oxford University Press, 1984), 23.
11. Paul Cavill, *Anglo-Saxon Christianity* (London: HarperCollins, 1999), 116.
12. Blair, 25.
13. Well, I was when I first wrote this. It was true *then*.

living memory. Further, the dates of Hygelac's raid and the beginning of the conversion process place the central events of *Beowulf* as the swan song of paganism. It is too easy for us to see that the Christian faith has not yet arrived in the world of *Beowulf*. Nevertheless, the first audience knew that it was just *about* to arrive, and that the world described in that poem was a world that was shortly to pass away. A comparable situation would be created if we were to compose an epic poem about Czar Nicolas. There is no way to hide from a modern audience the fact that the whole thing is about a man whose days and dynasty are numbered. Everyone would know about the great unspoken sequel.

Being on the verge of such a transformation would not be universally true for any given pagan tribe throughout the history of paganism. But in *this* poem, these were pagans on the verge of converting, whether they were aware of this or not (and they were not). Their historical context at that time was quite different from their own history several centuries before this, and from that of the other tribes that remained pagan for a long time afterwards. The pagan Frisians took Hygelac's life in 521 (when everyone in that region was a heathen), and in AD 755 they were *still* pagan when they murdered St. Boniface. In short, the Frisians were *not* on the threshold of conversion in this poem. But the central tribes in question were.

So some pagans were in transition, but not all of them. The life of freebooting piracy was one that appealed to many ancient pagan tribes. There are numerous accounts of many raiders throughout that ancient European world who entered into their piratical duties with enthusiasm and verve, never giving any of it a second thought. Speaking of the ancient Irish, Thomas Cahill notes, "The characters of the *Tain* do not think profoundly; they do not seem to think at all. But they do act—and with a characteristic panache and roundedness that easily convinces us of their humanity."[14] This is a humanity, all right, but it is not a *reflective* humanity. In short, there are many gen-

---

14. Thomas Cahill, *How the Irish Saved Civilization* (New York: Doubleday, 1995), 76.

erations of roistering pillagers who do not appear to think any other lifestyle is either possible or desirable. But in *Beowulf*, this lifestyle of raids and counter-raids, of vengeance accomplished and vengeance thwarted, is a way of life that is very evidently on its last legs. They are (most of them) heartily sick of it, and they keep trying to find ways of fixing the problems caused by the cycles of blood vengeance. Their vain attempts to weave peace, their frustrated attempts to stay the violence with the *wergild*, show that they know they have a serious problem. Their long-established way of doing things gives them all the civilization-building power of a biker gang. It is hard for us to imagine Viking angst, but I want to argue that the author of *Beowulf* is delivering us a vision of exactly that.

One other chronological note is worth mentioning. Hygelac dies circa 520, and Beowulf succeeds his son (who ruled only briefly) and then reigns for fifty years. This brings us down to the 570s, just a few decades before the Anglo-Saxons begin turning to the Christian faith. They are abandoned there by the poet (deliberately, I would argue) on the very threshold of conversion, like a waif left on the doorstep of an orphanage. The aesthetic impact of this is profound. Ovid taught us that it is art to conceal art. And so the poet has done this, but he has concealed it in much the same way that Poe's hero hid the purloined letter, by leaving it out in plain sight. The evangelistic and apologetic impact of this poem is not obvious, but only in the same way that the sky is not obvious.

At the end of the poem, the future is extremely dark, according to Wiglaf, and there is no hope whatever. The Geats now have tons of treasure and no king. Oh, good. Why would an intelligent Christian poet leave them there? The answer is that both he and his audience knew the sequel. And so do we, but perhaps we need to take a closer look at his timing. This poet really knows his business. Speaking of certain elements of the older heroic code and the new faith, Tolkien says this: "And in the poem I think we may observe not confusion, a half-hearted or a muddled business, but a fusion that has occurred at a given point of contact, between old and new, a product of thought and deep emotion."[15]

This fusion is not given to us in order to create a third way between the Christian faith and paganism. We can say this of the *Beowulf* poet—"one thing he knew clearly: those days were heathen—heathen, noble, and hopeless."[16] In this respect, I think that Martin Camargo gets it exactly right: "By linking that past to Old Testament history, by making clear that the hero is the best of men acting in strict accordance with the best rules of conduct then available to him, and finally by showing how far even this exemplary pagan's beliefs fall short of the Christian ideal, the poet instead forces his audience to recognize, and thence to abhor the lingering vestiges of paganism in their own hearts."[17]

In order to accomplish this, the poet has to treat certain issues very delicately. But this delicacy is for aesthetic reasons, and not because he is embarrassed by his faith. Rather, he is allowing his pagan characters to be embarrassed by *theirs*. What the *Beowulf* poet is doing is a powerful statement of his faith. But to make this statement, he has to show the characters sympathetically, so that a Christian audience cares what happens to them. At the same time, he has to show that they are in need of Christ and salvation—that which makes them sympathetic does not in any way earn them salvation. There is (probably) salvation for Beowulf himself, but this is an ambiguous hope, not stated clearly. The reasons for this should be become obvious shortly.

The poet gives us an interesting amalgam. The paganism with which we are asked to be in sympathy is more like the worldview of the Jews in the Old Testament than it is like that of the pagans of northern Europe. These noble pagans are monotheistic throughout; they are capable of backsliding into *crude* idolatry; they are well-versed in the ancient parts

---

15. J.R.R. Tolkien, *The Monsters and the Critics* (London: HarperCollins, 1997), 20.

16. Tolkien, 22.

17. Martin Camargo, "The Finn Episode and the Tragedy of Revenge in *Beowulf*," *Studies in Philology* 78, no. 5 (1981), 134.

of the *Old* Testament; they are totally oblivious to the name of Christ; they follow the Old Law (*ealde riht*); they have no priests in their midst, Christian or otherwise; and their culture, their way of life, marriage and war, is identical to that of their ancestors. But there is this one great difference: *they want out*—although they are not yet out.

It is important to emphasize that this kind of "paganism" did not really exist anywhere. In some respects, it is like both Beowulf and Melchizedek—without genealogy, father or mother, beginning of days or end of life.[18] Beowulf is an ahistorical character, surrounded by real-life, real-time historical characters. It is the same with the *religion* of Hrothgar and Beowulf—*that* did not exist anywhere either. This is a dramatic device. It enables a Christian audience to be sympathetic (which they would *not* be to paganism *tout court*), and at the same time it provides something to sympathize *with*. This culture is pagan enough to need Christ desperately, and not so pagan as to arouse the contempt of the audience. It is striking that in order to get this paganism "at its best," the *Beowulf* poet had to make it up, just as he had to make up a hero who exemplified all the heroic virtues. All the identifiable historical characters in this poem had significant flaws. The one king who does not is Beowulf, the one who cannot be found in the historical record anywhere else.

In this way, the poet is like Beowulf himself when he disdained to fight Grendel with a sword. The poet could have rejected paganism simply, dispatching it with the sword of the Spirit, in the name of Christ. But he does not use weapons—he grapples with paganism at its best, and tears off its right arm. But I am beginning to allegorize . . .

I said a moment ago that the worldview of this "pagan" society was more like that of the Jews in the Old Testament than it was like that of

18. I know, unlike Melchizedek, Beowulf does have a (minimal) genealogy. But it *is* minimal, and it is that way for a reason. Another point is worth remarking on: Beowulf is a dramatic and fictional character, not a mythological one. But even on the supposedly clear distinction between a historical character (like Hrothgar) and a mythological one (like his great-grandfather Shield), I must confess myself a dubious agnostic. I keep in mind Ambrose Bierce's wonderful definition of mythology, which is the "body of a primitive people's beliefs concerning its origin, early history, heroes, deities and so forth, as distinguished from the true accounts which it invents later." Ambrose Bierce, *The Devil's Dictionary* (New York: Dover Publications, 1958), 90.

real, live pillaging pagans. While this is true enough, it has to be noted that this is a comparative statement, and not a claim that Beowulf was at all Mosaic. The *ealde riht* mentioned as that law which Beowulf worries that he has violated (line 2332)[19] does not appear to be anything like the Ten Commandments.[20] Not only is there no specific mention of the New Testament in *Beowulf*, there is also no mention of any Old Testament book besides Genesis. And yet, *Beowulf* is filled with references to the book of Genesis. So this does not appear to be a contrast between natural revelation and special revelation. Rather, the pagans here have a very limited amount of special revelation, but what they *do* have, they refer to frequently. Cain is mentioned (108). The Flood is mentioned (1691). The giants that rebelled against God are mentioned (113).

In such a context, it seems reasonable to me to postulate that the *ealde riht* that Beowulf suddenly worries about after the dragon attack is the ancient Noahic covenant that was made just after the Flood, also from Genesis. After the Flood, God makes a covenant with all mankind (*not* just with the Jews). The rainbow is the sign of that covenant, and the terms of the covenant to be kept by man are found in that book as well. "And surely your blood of your lives will I require; at the hand of every beast will I require it, and at the hand of man; at the hand of every man's brother will I require the life of man. Whoso sheddeth man's blood, by man shall his blood be shed: for in the image of God made he man" (Genesis 9:5–6).

Beowulf, for all his nobility, is still a man of blood. Man is created in the *imago Dei*, and God will require it of us when we shed blood. It should be noted that Beowulf was not a murderer as Unferth was. Within the constraints of that society, Beowulf epitomized conformity to the heroic code. The indictment that the poet is handing down here is not

---

19. Unless otherwise noted, all line numbers are from this edition.
20. It also does not seem to me to be anything like the medieval understanding of "natural law." Natural law is *timeless*, and this law is *ancient*. And Beowulf seems to be as unlike Boethius as a man can be.

against Beowulf as an individual. As an individual, he was noble indeed, and no murderer. But the society that he represented (*and* Grendel, *and* the dragon) was a murderous society. And it is that culture that receives the indictment. For example, Beowulf as an individual does not grasp at the throne, even when Hygd offers it to him. He is not in this for himself. Nevertheless, the reason she was offering it to him in the first place was that her husband had gone off on an ill-advised smash and grab run to Friesland, *and Beowulf had gone with him* (2356–2361). Of course, it was his duty to do so, and that was the dilemma. He is a good man trapped in an evil system, and it is a system from which he cannot extricate himself.

The problem is that this warrior society, for all its emphasis on honor and fealty, had created a culture which necessarily established treachery at the heart of it. This is the meaning of both Grendel and Grendel's mother. Grendel is treachery embodied, and Grendel's mother is the mother of that treachery, the mother of all treachery. This point is made over and over, and in numerous ways.

First, Grendel is descended from Cain, the first fratricide. Cain is therefore the father of Grendel, and, in turn, in a very real sense Grendel as kinslayer is the father of this whole society. Grendel is both outside and inside the mead-hall. He doesn't belong there (and he is not there by day) and he cannot touch the throne there, but at night he has the run of the place (167–170). In this respect, as a twisted "human," Grendel is *not* like the dragon at the end of the poem—which is more of a force of nature to be reckoned with, like an earthquake. And yet, the dragon clearly represents something about this society as well, as we shall see.

As a descendent of Cain, Grendel is also descended from Adam and Eve. He knows he belongs to the human race, and yet his bitter hatred and envy eat at him like a canker. He belongs in, and yet cannot be in. This can only mean that when he comes in (which he *has* to do, being one of them), he comes in to destroy.

Grendel corresponds in many ways to the society that he hates. He is a fratricide, and kin-slaying in that ancient world, whether we are talking about kin by blood or kin by law, is tragically common. We see this in how Unferth is welcome at Hrothgar's court even though he took the blood of his own relatives (588–590). We see this in the Lay of Finn, where Hildeburh lost both brother and son, who were on opposing sides of a blood feud (1117–1120). We see it in Beowulf's prediction of what will happen to the attempt at peace-weaving with Freawaru (2059–2064). We see it in how Beowulf and his father came to Heorot when Beowulf was a boy—Hrothgar paid the *wergild* so that Ecgtheow would not be held responsible for one of his slayings (472). We see it in Wealhtheow's concern that her sons will be killed by their cousin Hrothulf (1182–1185), just as one of them actually was. So Grendel is descended from a man who took the life of his brother. So? How does this set him apart? Who cares about *that* around these parts?

Another connection can be seen in the parity between Beowulf and Grendel. In his first raid on Heorot, Grendel snatches thirty men (122). When Beowulf comes against Grendel, he does so with the grip of thirty men (381–382). When Beowulf returns from the fight with the Frisians, he brings back thirty suits of armor (2363). Beowulf really does fight Grendel, but when he does so, it is represented to us as a civil war, *a contest between peers*. Further, it is portrayed for us as a civil war that Beowulf cannot ultimately win.

While there is no way I would want to be mistaken for a Freudian, I think there is something here that must be reckoned with. To see Beowulf and Grendel as engaged in internecine strife does not obligate us to take it in an individualistic way. We may make this point and yet escape the Freudian depths of the murky subconscious if we take it as an objective cultural struggle and not a subjective individual one. Niles compares the two approaches:

> Grendel is taken to be Beowulf's shadow self. The physical combat between these two fearsome opponents is taken to represent an inner struggle between two opposed psychic principles, one of which is associated with our moral being, the other with

those dark impulses that civilized people normally suppress (Freud's ego or superego and id, respectively, whether or not these terms are invoked). To approach *Beowulf* in this manner is to read its action as a psychomachia whereby fearsome antisocial impulses threaten to overwhelm consciousness but are ultimately overcome and integrated into an expanded self. Foley (1977) takes this argument and converts it to communal history: the integration in question was a cultural one for the Anglo-Saxons as a people.[21]

For my money, Foley takes it running away. This is a broad cultural issue, and Grendel is as much a part of it as Beowulf is. But to represent this epic poem as a portrayal of the internal subjective struggles of a narcissistic modern is as anachronistic and foolish as to start looking for Beowulf's inner child. The poet is addressing a problem which this people as a people knew they had. A poem like this should not be used as a blank screen on which we may project problems that we know *we* have. Maybe Hrothgar was actually worried about global warming or high cholesterol.

Still another link is seen in the fact that Hrothgar pays the *wergild* for the Geat warrior that Grendel ate (1055–1056). Why would he be responsible to do that unless in some sense the Danes were responsible for the death? And how could they be responsible without being identified in some way with Grendel? He was a monster all right, but he was *their* monster.

The symbolism of how Grendel dies is also very important. Beowulf does not kill him outright with the sword, but rather grapples with him barehanded. The end result is that Beowulf tears off Grendel's right arm, and Grendel lopes off in pain in order to die *somewhere else*. Beowulf is distressed by the fact that he did not kill Grendel there in the hall (962–963). He consequently did not have a carcass to show Hrothgar. If treachery had been slain where it actually manifested itself—in Heorot—the problem would have been symbolically solved. But this victory at Heorot provided only a respite, not a final victory. This is why the mother of

---

21. John D. Niles in "Myth and History" as found in *A Beowulf Handbook* (Lincoln, NE: University of Nebraska Press, 1997), 223.

treachery comes back the next night to seek her revenge—but even when she is also slain, and the head of Grendel is brought back to the hall, the implied statement is clear: All this is still insufficient. Grendel's mother is slain in her lair, the same place where Grendel died, and so treachery is *not* slain within the walls of Heorot.

In the victory party right afterwards, Wealhtheow is righteously maneuvering in order to protect her two sons from their cousin (1190–1194). She seats Beowulf between Hrethric and Hrothmund, in order that he might protect them from whom? From Grendel? Someone might object that Grendel is dead. Not really.

Another argument for the importance of these monsters as human treachery (and the impotence of the heroic code in the face of that treachery) can be seen in the chiastic structure of *Beowulf*. The fitts of *Beowulf* can be understood as forming a chiasm, a chiasm that helps us identify this as a central theme of the poem. The central fitt of the poem is the one in which Grendel's mother is pursued to her lair. While much more could be said about this aspect of the poem, the point can be illustrated by the two fitts on either side of this central point. In the first, Grendel's mother takes revenge by killing a warrior in Heorot (Fitt 19). Here we are again, killing people in the fellowship mead hall. In the next, Hrothgar despairs and talks (20). In the central fitt, Beowulf pursues the monster to her lair (21). She is pursued in this fitt, *and not killed*. In the next fitt, Beowulf fights with Grendel's mother (22), and this is the counterpart to Hrothgar's despairing talk. What is the link between the fitts? Hrothgar talks and Beowulf fights. But then the next fitt reveals even more. In this section (23), Beowulf actually kills Grendel's mother in her cave, just as in the corresponding fitt *she* had killed Aeschere in Heorot.[22] The two events should be seen as a stark contrast, but in some respects

---

22. Further documentation on this can be found in my next essay, "Chiastic Structure in *Beowulf*." An actual *scholarly* documentation can be found in John D. Niles, "Ring Composition and the Structure of Beowulf" PMLA 94, no. 5 (Oct. 1979), 924–935. Niles does not address the issue of the fitts at all, but he shows how ring composition is integral to the poem, and the points drawn out in his article are generally consistent with the conclusions I drew.

they are still comparable. The central point of this poem is emphasized by all this, however: in *this* society homes and halls are for killing in.[23]

Another significant aspect of this apologetic is that the *Beowulf* poet goes out of his way to honor and admire a class of aristocratic warriors who are, at the same time, utterly and entirely impotent, which is not what you want from your warriors. They can kill just about anything, *but they cannot kill what is destroying their people.* They cannot kill the cycle of violence and destruction, and any attempt to do so only fuels it further. The heroic code turns out to be the ultimate tar baby.

The central representative of this is Hrothgar. He was a magnificent warrior in his day (1680), and his prowess in battle was unquestioned. The poet goes out of his way to say that Hrothgar's valor cannot be challenged (1041–1044). And yet, his impotence in this regard is underlined time and again. The morning after Grendel is killed, Hrothgar receives the good news and comes out to look at the grisly arm. He comes, a great warrior king, having spent the night in a warm bed with Wealhtheow, and when he comes, he advances with a troop of maidens following him (922–926), a bevy of curvaceous thanes. And when his warriors are rejoicing over Beowulf's prowess, the poet tells us that they did not think to criticize Hrothgar. Why did he tell us this? The answer is obviously that the circumstances invited such criticism. Hrothgar did not fight as Beowulf did (or even as Beowulf did later on against the dragon when *he* was an old man). Usually kings are very prickly about such comparisons, and yet Hrothgar still honors Beowulf highly.[24]

At the same time, when Hrothgar speaks of how he built up his kingdom through his courage on the battlefield over the period of many years, no one hoots at him. They all knew it was true. He had been a great

---

23. The point is plain here (and other chiastic patterns in *Beowulf* reinforce it as well).
    A Grendel's mother kills Aeschere where he sleeps
      B Hrothgar despairs and talks
        C Beowulf pursues Grendel's mother
      B′ Beowulf fights with Grendel's mother
    A′ Beowulf kills Grendel's mother where she sleeps
24. "Saul has slain his thousands, and David his tens of thousands."

warrior indeed, and no one questions this, least of all the poet. It would not make the poet's point to have Hrothgar fail his people because he was a cowardly king who would not fight. No, he was a true warrior, and he saw about fifty years earlier than Beowulf did how useless this was. If Hrothgar had never been a fine warrior-king, then a defender of this way of life could reply to the poet that *this* was the problem—"If Hrothgar had only done his duty . . ." But he *had* done his duty. He had done everything expected of him. He established his people, and this meant that he enriched his people by warring with others and successfully robbing them.[25] When he settles down to enjoy the success of this, Grendel arrives to start devouring Danes. The hopelessness of this situation can be seen even in the smallest details of the poem. Chickering notes, "Clark argues convincingly that, throughout the poem, arms and armor symbolize the ambiguities at the heart of the heroic vision."[26]

All this relates to one other aspect of the poem. I argued earlier that the culture we are considering is pagan, but pagan just on the verge of conversion. If Hrothgar is a type of this society (and I think it is clear that he is), another way of seeing this is that paganism here is infirm through old age. Just as Hrothgar had once "done his duty" with enthusiasm, so this pagan society had once embraced the heroic code with the same kind of enthusiasm. But old age brings perspective, at least in some instances. Here we see that both Hrothgar and the culture around him have come to see that all they had attained was vanity and striving after wind.

The motive of Grendel in his treachery was envy. He wanted to be inside Heorot in order to be able to enjoy the creation song of the *scop*, and yet at the same time he hated the creation song of the *scop*. In the dragon, we

---

25. The Christian take on this kind of thing is illustrated in *The City of God*, where Augustine tells us (approvingly) the story of the pirate who was brought up before the emperor. The pirate asked why he was considered a pirate for doing to *ships* what the emperor did to *countries*. I forget what happened to the witty pirate then.

26. Chickering, *Beowulf*, 297. In other words, the tension between heroism and despair extends even into the *description* of armor and weapons. See also George Clark's original article, "Beowulf's Armor," *English Literary History* 32, no. 4 (December, 1965), 416-19.

find the other basic driving engine of this culture—greed. While Grendel did have stuff in his lair, it is clear that plunder was not really his motive. He would raid Heorot in order to eat people, and not to take their gold. His motives were malice, hatred, envy, and all the rest of that rancid bouquet.

But this dragon has a heart full of *greed*. He comes upon the lost treasure of a vanished people, and takes up residence there. After a long period of time, a runaway slave from the Geats finds his way into the dragon's barrow by accident. As he leaves, he does what every self-respecting Viking would do with someone else's stuff—he takes it. He takes just one cup, in order to pay off his master, but he takes it. This is an entire society that bases its economy on pillaging. Whatever generosity a king might display in being a ring-giver was a generosity that was fueled by raiding other tribes and taking what they had. The tribe that had first gathered this treasure had no doubt done it in just this way. Then a dragon comes and sleeps on top of that stash for years. A slave comes and takes one cup. But what does it matter that it is only one cup? He comes and he *takes*. That is what he does because that is what everyone does. And what happens next is what always happens next.

The dragon flies out in a rage—which is what every robbed tribe would also do—and he seeks his revenge. The externality of the dragon represents the fact that when another tribe sets sail to come against yours, there is no reasoning with it. This is just the way it is. Grendel represents that which would provoke a protest—Hrothulf ought not to have done what he did to Hrethric. Unferth ought not to have done what he did to his kin. It still happens, but treachery always calls forth a greater outrage. The malevolence of Grendel is hot, like malice always is. The rage of the dragon is cold, like the gold it is acquiring or defending. The dragon hates, but it is nothing personal. Grendel hates, and everything about it is personal. With the dragon, killing is a means to an end. With Grendel, killing is the end itself. The dragon is a night-flying outsider. Grendel is a cannibal. So this society is surrounded—hot enmity within and cold enmity without.

The dragon clearly represents the cold, pragmatic *quid pro quo* of an economy that was driven by the five-fingered discount. The last survivor laments the whole process, and puts the treasure in a barrow to await the coming of the dragon (2269–2272). After the dragon is killed, Wiglaf laments the whole process, just like the last survivor (and the chiastic structure, as well as Beowulf's word, shows us that Wiglaf is *also* a last survivor[27]). The Geats put the treasure in a barrow (with Beowulf) to await the coming of the Swedes. This obviously puts the Swedes in the position of a "dragon." The churl who takes the cup does so to give it to his lord, who receives it gladly (2285–2288). This is just what every loyal thane would do, coming back from the wars, and it was no doubt something just like this that had provoked the Swedes. The fight with the dragon is even described in terms of a feud (2289).

This is where the poem brings us, in order to abandon us there. What can be done to save this people from their lost condition? By the end of the poem, it is absolutely certain that there is nothing that the people of this culture can do about their *lostness*. When they worship idols, they are depraved. When they win a great battle, they take the wealth of others. When they seek to repair the damage that this victorious pillaging caused, they will give a princess as a peace-weaver. But at the wedding reception some old guy will see the wrong sword on the wrong hip, and the young warrior wearing it will be swanking around like he *wants* to be killed. And if a great hero arrives from nowhere to lead the people, he can only lead them deeper into *these* traditions. Shield Sheafson drifted to the Danes in a boat—what could be more of a sign? And yet he was only able to establish them more firmly in the ways of blood. Beowulf came to the Geats, and he gave them a fifty-year respite. But even he could not deliver them.

Beowulf is not a Christ figure, although the temptation to read him this way is understandable. He delivers the people (temporarily). He descends into hell, just like in the Apostles' Creed. He is a noble and

---

27   Niles, "Ring Composition," 928.

high-minded hero. He fights against wickedness and the forces of the devil. He sacrifices his life. His thanes all scatter except for Wiglaf, who is the apostle John. But I take all these similarities as ways of pointing to an almost-Christ, or, as I said in my title, the *unChrist*.

Alcuin notwithstanding, Beowulf appears to be saved as an individual. But this is not stated outright, although the hints are there. Beowulf tells Unferth that he is going to hell for his kin-slaying (589). This would be odd if there were no distinction between Beowulf and Unferth in the afterlife. Grendel also dies and goes to hell (854). But if Beowulf is going to follow Grendel there, then what was the point of all the fighting *here*? The poet says that when Shield Sheafson died, he (a noble lord) went *on Frean wære*, into "the keeping of the Lord" (27). And at the end of *Beowulf*, it says that Beowulf died and went to "seek the doom of the just"—*sawol secean soð-fæstra dom* (2822).[28] But although we may be fairly certain of all this, the argument for it is still oblique. The poet doesn't insult his Christian audience (or provoke them) by having Beowulf ascend into the presence of Christ and the saints, with angels singing all around. At the same time, we are invited to believe that he is *not* going to the place of torment.

Now if the *Beowulf* poet only hints that Beowulf is saved, how much less is he presenting him as a savior? The "salvation" that Beowulf brings is by no means everlasting. This means that Beowulf, the best and noblest that paganism could offer, one who would even probably be blessed somehow in the afterlife, could still not provide salvation for his people. That would have to await the arrival of another "hero," entirely unmentioned in the poem. If Hrothgar is the penultimate Viking hero, Beowulf is the ultimate Viking hero. And yet everything they do still comes to nothing, and *must* come to nothing. The true hero who is standing just off stage as the poem ends is Christ. He is the savior/hero, and everyone who first heard this poem was expecting Him, and was worked over by the poem to *long* for Him. But it cannot be emphasized too strongly that this

---

28. These two translations are Chickering's.

coming Christ was a different *kind* of hero, one who conquers by dying, and not by killing.

To conclude and summarize my argument, I would say this. First, Grendel should be understood as a dark and necessary aspect of this noble and aristocratic society. So long as this warrior code of honor is the organizing principle of a culture, that culture will be haunted by Grendels somehow, someway. Secondly, the establishment of a warrior ruling caste necessarily creates an enemy of the society which the warriors are dedicated to defend, but it is an enemy which they cannot defend against. The epitome of this is Hrothgar and also, in another (superior) way, Beowulf. The warriors with their code of honor cannot defend their people against the necessary ramifications of that code of honor whenever it is applied. In the immortal words of Pogo, "We have met the enemy, and he is us." Third, a society turned on itself in this way is not capable of fighting external enemies to a satisfactory conclusion—especially when the dragon represents the baser motives of that whole culture. Grendel is the problem within each tribe; the dragon is the problem of all the other tribes. And after you have considered the dilemma both inside and the outside, what else is there?

In another setting, the death of a dragon (and the recovery of mountains of gold) would be unqualified good news. But in this setting, the recovery of all the dragon's gold would have presented a very serious problem for the Geats even if Beowulf had not been killed. This external threat is removed, and yet this victory simply creates additional problems with all the surrounding tribes, all the other external threats. The dragon was a very satisfactory enemy, placed in such a way that whether he lives or dies, the future of the Geats is very grim indeed. And so even though the dragon of greed dies, so does Beowulf, and the gold is still there to beckon other dragons.

This is a people who would be quite eager to hear a preaching monk. And I cannot imagine that a king like Wiglaf would turn such a monk away.

Chiastic Structure in *Beowulf*

INTRODUCTION

Some scholars have mentioned in passing that there are some chiastic elements in *Beowulf*. For example, the poem opens and closes with a funeral. Then I once heard it mentioned that nobody pays much attention to the fitts, whatever they are. This was invitation enough for me, and so I decided to examine the structure of *Beowulf* according to certain themes found within the fitts and see if it followed a chiastic structure. The answer is that I believe so. At the very least, I believe that what I have uncovered merits further study. It is quite possible we have not seen anything like this since the days of Wald the Woingas. (Since I saw his name in *Widsith*, I knew I just had to work it in somehow.)

BACKGROUND

Chesterton remarked somewhere that a courageous man ought to be willing to attack any error, no matter how old—but that there were some errors too old to be patronized.

A variant of this was Tolkien's objection to many of the critics of *Beowulf* in his day, and it appears to me that in some senses the criticism still applies. Certain critics have in many ways patronized this poem, neglecting to take it on its own terms. They have not looked at the elements of the poem *as it has come to us*. But perhaps a good starting assumption is that everything is there and in its place for a reason, and then to use that as a basis for seeking to understand it.

> I would express the whole industry in yet another allegory. A man inherited a field in which was an accumulation of old stone, part of an older hall. Of the old stone some had already been used in building the house in which he actually lived, not far from the old house of his fathers. Of the rest he took some and built a tower. But his friends coming perceived at once (without troubling to climb the steps) that these stones had formerly belonged to a more ancient building. So they pushed the tower over, with no little labour, in order to look for hidden carvings and inscriptions, or to discover whence the man's distant forefathers had obtained the building material. Some suspecting a deposit of coal under the soil began to dig for it, and forgot even the stones. They all said, "This tower is most interesting." But they also said (after pushing it over): "What a muddle it is in!" And even the man's own descendants, who might have been expected to consider what he had been about, were heard to murmur: "He is such an odd fellow! Imagine his using these old stones just to build a nonsensical tower! Why did not he restore the old house? He had no sense of proportion." But from the top of that tower the man had been able to look out upon the sea.[29]

POETIC ARCHITECTURE

One of the possibilities that I would like us to consider is that the fitts are stones, and that they provide an architectural structure that was common in the ancient world. Although frequently invisible to moderns, the chiasm was readily identifiable throughout the ancient world, and was *extremely* common in Scripture—a source that was obviously well known to the author of *Beowulf*. Consider this example from Jeremiah 2:27–28:

> In the time of their trouble they say,
>> "Arise and save us!"
>>> But where are your gods that you made for yourself?
>> Let them arise, if they can save you,
> In the time of your trouble.

---

29 Tolkien, 8–9.

But we might have trouble in a modern setting with modern examples.

> My wife is a good woman; her kindness to me is sure and unfailing. When I am discouraged, she picks me up; whenever I slip her counsel sustains me. She really is steady in her character. Her goodness is quite remarkable.

Asked to outline this, we would probably not do it like this:

> My wife is a good woman;
>   her kindness to me is sure and unfailing.
>   When I am discouraged, she picks me up;
>   whenever I slip her counsel sustains me.
>   She really is steady in her character.
> Her goodness is quite remarkable.

The problem for us here is that we impose our forms (or lack of them) on ancient texts, as in Tolkien's allegory. But in the ancient world, there were short chiasms like the above, and there were book-length chiasms. Getting used to this obviously requires a certain way of seeing.

FITTS AND STARTS

According to my calculations, the average number of lines per fitt (for those who like to keep up on such things) is somewhere between seventy-three and seventy-four. But some of them are as short as forty-two and some are as long as 141.

Just one other word about the numbering of these fitts. There are forty-three of them, which means we have our odd number that the chiasm requires. But because nothing in this life is simple, and because one of our *Beowulf* scribes was possibly a screw-up, the first fitt is unnumbered, and the numbering starts with the second one. But then, late in the poem, the realization comes (to the *second* scribe?) that everything is one off, and so he helps us jump over 30, putting us back on track to end on 43.

The diagram on pages 134–135 shows the overall chiastic structure of the poem. The line numbers and the length of each fitt are noted as well as the original fitt numbers (in Roman numerals) and my renumbering (in Arabic numerals).

DIAGRAM: The Chiastic Structure of *Beowulf*

Chiasm line number — Summary of fitt content	Line numbers (line count)	Original fitt #	New fitt #
1 — Funeral of Shield	1–52 (52 lines)	—	1
2 — Hrothgar rises, Grendel stirs	53–114 (61 lines)	I	2
3 — Grendel kills thirty men, Heorot is deserted	115–190 (75 lines)	II	3
4 — Hrothgar broods, Beowulf sails and meets the coast guard	191–259 (68 lines)	III	4
5 — Beowulf answers the coast guard	260–321 (61 lines)	IV	5
6 — Beowulf and Wulfgar	322–372 (50 lines)	V	6
7 — Hrothgar and Beowulf meet, "Fate must go as it must"	373–456 (83 lines)	VI	7
8 — Hrothgar's speech and welcome	457–499 (42 lines)	VII	8
9 — Unferth and Beowulf clash	500–559 (59 lines)	VIII	9
10 — Sea creatures, Unferth silenced, vow to Wealhtheow	560–662 (102 lines)	IX	10
11 — Asleep in Heorot, Beowulf trusts God	663–710 (47 lines)	X	11
12 — Grendel is disturbed and advances	711–792 (81 lines)	XI	12
13 — Fight with Grendel	793–838 (45 lines)	XII	13
14 — Giddy retainers, story of Heremod	839–926 (87 lines)	XIII	14
15 — Hrothgar views arm, Beowulf wishes he had corpse	927–992 (65 lines)	XIV	15
16 — Heorot refurbished	993–1051 (58 lines)	XV	16
17 — Beowulf rewarded, "Lay of Finn" begins	1052–1126 (74 lines)	XVI	17
18 — Hengest plots revenge, Wealhtheow plans	1127–1193 (66 lines)	XVII	18
19 — Gifts bestowed on Beowulf	1194–1252 (58 lines)	XVIII	19
20 — Grendel's mother kills in Heorot	1253–1322 (69 lines)	XIX	20
21 — Hrothgar despairs and talks	1323–1384 (61 lines)	XX	21

Parallels Teased Out

It needs to be acknowledged at the outset that I am stating various themes within the fitts while looking for patterns or contrasts, and I am looking for things that are centered around the grand themes that have been manifest in the poem—honor, treachery, the hopelessness of this freebooting manner of life, etc. I have put in bold those pairs that I think are particularly strong, and have phrased everything accordingly. I have put in italics those I think are moderately strong. I have wanted to guard against "projecting," because I know it is quite possible to be a little too creative here. And besides, maybe God puts chiasms everywhere—Atlantic coast, Appalachians, Great Plains, Rockies, Pacific coast. Maybe chiasms are like driveway gravel, I don't know.

1   **Funeral of Shield**
1´   **Funeral of Beowulf**

2   *Trouble from Grendel looms*
2´   *Trouble from cursed treasure looms*

3   *Grendel kills thirty men, Heorot is deserted*
3´   *Hygelac kills Ongentheow, Geatland will be deserted*

4   **Hrothgar broods**
4´   **Wiglaf broods**

5   **The coast guard speaks of the difference between words and deeds**
5´   **Wiglaf speaks of the difference between words and deeds**

6   *Beowulf arrives and is introduced by name*
6´   *Beowulf departs in death*

7   *Hrothgar and Beowulf meet, "Fate must go as it must"*
7´   *Wiglaf and Beowulf kill the dragon, and see the gold*

8   *Hrothgar's speech and Beowulf welcomed*
8´   *Wiglaf's speech and Beowulf wounded*

9   **Beowulf reminisces**
9´   **Beowulf reminisces**

10   *Vow to Wealhtheow*
10´   *Beowulf hunts dragon in sorrow and despair*

11	Beowulf trusts God
11′	Beowulf believes he offended God
12	Grendel is disturbed and advances
12′	Dragon is disturbed and advances
13	*Beowulf fights with Grendel*
13′	*Beowulf does not fight with Hygelac*
14	Story of Heremod
14′	Story of Ingeld
15	*Beowulf has bad feeling about not having corpse*
15′	*Beowulf has bad feeling about Freawaru*
16	Heorot refurbished
16′	Geatland refurbished
17	Beowulf receives gifts
17′	Beowulf prepares to leave with gifts
18	*Wealhtheow plans*
18′	*Hrothgar admonishes*
19	*Beowulf keeps gifts*
19′	*Beowulf keeps hilt*
20	Grendel's mother kills in Heorot
20′	Beowulf kills Grendel's mother in her lair
21	Hrothgar talks
21′	Beowulf fights
22	(CENTER) Pursuit of Grendel's mother

One of the things I would want to urge modern students of this classic to consider is the aesthetic value of structure and rhythm. Aspects of these values are sadly neglected in our day, almost to the point where they are entirely invisible to us. Chiasm, when it is used well, is not hidden the way a code is hidden, or a message in invisible ink. Rather, a chiasm is hidden the way a skeleton is hidden—but without that framework holding everything up, the words on the surface of the text would not have nearly the force that they do. *Beowulf* is a powerful poem, and the chiastic structure is a good part of the reason.

ACKNOWLEDGEMENTS

I need to thank a number of people for the practical help and encouragement they gave to this project in various ways. First, I want to thank Dr. Rick Fehrenbacher for a most stimulating class in Anglo-Saxon and *Beowulf*. I also need to thank my father, Jim Wilson, for his willingness to serve as a reader. Bekah Merkle's fantastic input saved me from at least one howler. I am greatly indebted to Valerie Bost for her help in what must have been a nightmare of punctuation. Any renegade commas that remain are, of course, my own. I need to thank Nancy always for everything. And many thanks go to the visionary crew at the new Canon Press—Forrest Dickison, James Engerbretson, Brian Kohl, and, of course, Nate Wilson and Aaron Rench.